WHO KILLED CONSTABLE COCK?

ALSO BY ANGELA BUCKLEY

The Real Sherlock Holmes: The Hidden Story of Jerome Caminada

The Victorian Supersleuth Investigates series:

Amelia Dyer and the Baby Farm Murders

WHO KILLED CONSTABLE COCK?

A VICTORIAN TRUE CRIME MURDER CASE

by Angela Buckley

Angela Buckley

Paperback ISBN: 978-0-9935640-2-4
Ebook ISBN: 978-0-9935640-3-1

Published by Manor Vale Associates

6 Merthyr Vale
Reading RG4 8QQ

For my parents

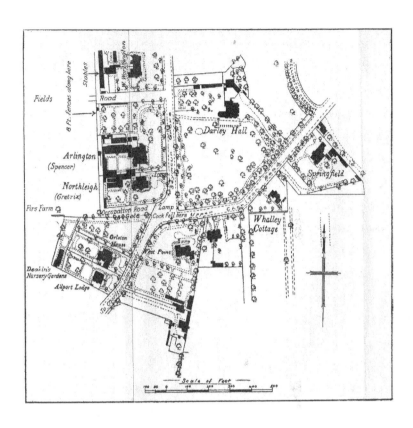

Fields

Stables

8 Ft. Fences along here

W. Washington Road

Arlington
(Spencer)

Northleigh
(Gretrix)

Firs Farm

Occupation Road

Gate

Lamp

Darley Hall

Springfield

Cock fell here

Whalley
Cottage

Orleton
House

West Point

Deakin's
Nursery Gardens

Allport Lodge

Scale of Feet

100 50 0   100   200   300   400   500

Contents

Preface

There is no place like home and, although I left Manchester at the age of 18 to study in London, I still feel deeply connected to my city, and it is one of my favourite places to research and write about. I grew up in Old Trafford, on the edge of Chorlton-cum-Hardy. It was a reasonably quiet district in the 1970s and 1980s – much more so than the city centre, or Moss Side where I went to school. However, a century earlier, it had been the scene of a shocking murder, which took place just near my family home.

On 1 August 1876, PC Nicholas Cock was walking his beat at midnight. He had reached the junction of West Point, where he stopped to chat with a colleague, when two shots rang out in the dark. The young police officer took a bullet to the chest and, shortly after, died of his injuries. His superior officer, Superintendent Bent, knew exactly who the culprits were and instantly set out to frame them for his constable's murder. This fascinating case led to a murder conviction, a startling twist and an astonishing confession by a notorious burglar.

Using contemporary newspaper accounts and the original trial records, I am re-telling this case in full detail for the first time in 140 years. I have visited PC Cock's grave and many of the places that feature in our shared history in Chorlton. This was my home too, and I feel privileged to have an opportunity to share Constable Cock's tragic story.

Angela Buckley
Reading, 2017

Chapter 1

'THE LITTLE BOBBY'

'The circumstances of the sad affair are at
present enshrouded to some extent in mystery,
but...the deed has been coolly and deliberately
planned.'

(Manchester Courier, 3 August 1876)

1 August 1876

There was very little moonlight as the young police officer set
out from the village of Chorlton-cum-Hardy in Manchester. The
night was cloudy but dry, and large trees overhung the deserted
pathways as he followed his regular beat. After passing the fields
of a local nursery, he made his way along Manchester Road
towards the junction of West Point, a small grassy triangle in
the middle of three main thoroughfares. A pleasant, tree-lined
suburb of large residential houses and extensive gardens, its
wealthy residents were in their beds, safely locked away from
plunderers and prowlers from the lawless metropolis nearby.

As he walked, 21-year-old PC Nicholas Cock overtook
John Massey Simpson, a law student who was on his way
home after spending a convivial evening with a friend. They
continued together to the 'jutting stone', which marked the

boundary of Cock's route. Described in the local press as 'dark and lonesome', it was a meeting place for police constables to exchange information and pass on messages. At just before midnight, the men stopped to chat for a few minutes and were briefly joined by PC James Beanland, before they all went their separate ways.

John Simpson turned away from the junction, down Upper Chorlton Road, heading towards his home near Manley Hall, a large villa built for a wealthy textiles merchant. Simpson had walked just 150 yards when two shots rang out in quick succession, followed immediately by cries of 'Murder, murder! Oh, I'm shot!' The student ran back to the junction as fast as he could and found PC Cock lying on the footpath, near a garden wall, while PC Beanland was blowing his whistle to call for assistance. Raising the prostrate police officer up from the ground, Simpson saw blood spurting from a wound in his chest.

Two more officers arrived having heard the shots, while walking their beat on Seymour Grove, one of the main roads leading to the junction. PC Beanland bent down and cradled his colleague's head, as Simpson unfastened his tunic. Seeing the extent of the fallen officer's injuries, PC Beanland called out to two night soil men returning from Manchester after emptying the privies. The men placed PC Cock into one of their carts and conveyed him straight to the doctor's surgery, a short distance along Upper Chorlton Road. A surgeon, who was summoned to assist, pronounced the young officer's chances as 'hopeless', as the bullet had penetrated his right lung, causing heavy blood loss. Suffering from respiratory difficulties and severe chest pain, the police officer was laid on the sofa and given brandy, in an attempt to revive his spirits and numb the pain but, at 1.10 am, despite the doctors' efforts, Nicholas Cock died.

When news of the shooting reached Old Trafford police station, the senior officer had just retired to bed. On hearing the night bell, he got up immediately and asked the officer on duty what the matter was, who replied, 'Cock is shot.' Without a moment's delay, Superintendent Bent went to Dr Dill's surgery, arriving about 1 am, too late to help his junior officer. He watched helplessly as PC Cock breathed his last.

~~~

Nicholas Cock was born in 1856 in Cornwall. He was the youngest of nine children, with four brothers and four sisters. By the time he was born, his brother, also named Nicholas, had died aged eight, of 'brain disease', which could have been meningitis. His father, Nicholas senior, was a lead and copper miner, and both he and his wife Elizabeth were illiterate.

The Cock family lived in the villages near St Ive, not far from Liskeard. In 1861 they were living in Middlehill, where the two oldest sons both worked down the mine and a daughter, 20-year-old Maria, was employed as a copper dresser, which involved washing and sorting the ore after it had been extracted. Six years later, 59-year-old Nicholas senior died of dropsy, swelling caused by kidney or heart disease. Young Nicholas was just 11 years old.

By the beginning of the 1870s, teenage Nicholas was also working as a copper miner and lodging with his sister Elizabeth and her husband. As the decade wore on, many Cornish mines closed and, like thousands of other miners, Nicholas lost his job. He then moved to Durham, where he found employment as a collier with a large mining engineering firm. Just before Christmas in 1875, at the age of 20, he joined the Lancashire Constabulary, formed in 1839.

Prior to 1839 the Lancashire boroughs had been policed by local constables until, following the Municipal Corporation Act of 1835, a single county force was created. Initially 502 officers policed a population of almost a million. In the early decades of the nineteenth century, the county had a high crime rate, with more arrests than in most other parts of the country. Throughout 1836 alone, just over 2,500 individuals were tried for serious offences at the county sessions and assizes courts. Eighty-nine per cent of trials were for theft.

In 1875, a constable earned between 24 and 28 shillings a week, depending on his class and length of service. This was a similar income to industrial workers, such as warehousemen, tanners and rope-makers, but double that of a general labourer. This was a step up for Nicholas Cock, who obviously aspired to more than working down the mines or physical labour.

PC Cock wore the customary dark blue buttoned tunic, with

the collar numerals 1015, and a 'coxcomb' helmet, with a bronze badge bearing a Lancashire rose. The new-style 'coxcomb' helmets were first introduced by the Metropolitan Police in 1863, replacing the high top hat. They were so called because of a ridge that ran down the back of the helmet. Firearms and cutlasses were not standard issue to police constables, and so PC Cock was armed only with a staff. He also carried a whistle on a chain to alert his colleagues in emergencies.

The young police officer was 5 feet 7 1/2 inches tall, which was two inches taller than the average height for a man in 1876. He had grey eyes, brown hair and a pale complexion. Assigned to Chorlton-cum-Hardy police station, he was a strong man, of medium stature but 'very powerfully built'. Known locally as the 'Little Bobby', because of his youth, he had a reputation for sticking to the rules. Some locals found him officious and even 'zealous' in his pursuit of law breakers. On his death, the local press stated equivocally that 'on the whole (he) had conducted himself well.'

In the early hours of 2 August 1876, after hearing the news of PC Cock's murder, Superintendent Bent instantly suspected the identity of his killers. With his prime suspects firmly in his sights, and without considering any other leads, he set out to prove their guilt.

Chapter 2

A MURDER OF A DASTARDLY CHARACTER

'As naturally might be expected the occurrence created great sensation, not only in the immediate neighbourhood, but throughout the whole city.'

(Manchester Courier, 3 August 1876)

Chorlton-cum-Hardy is a suburb of Manchester, four and a half miles south-west of the city centre, now characterised by small shops, street cafés and delicatessens. Originally a rural village of wattle and daub cottages with thatched roofs, the tranquil farming community was surrounded by fields and meadows, with brooks running through them, and cultivated areas with nursery gardens. There were workers' cottages, farms and some large estates with grand residences, such as the former home of the Mosleys at Hough End Hall, an Elizabethan manor house. Apart from agriculture, local people were engaged in hand loom weaving, which was carried out mostly at home. Many women were in domestic service. Residents also worked in the marl and brick pits throughout the area. Marl was a lime-rich mudstone, used on the fields as fertiliser. Since the construction of the Duke of Bridgewater's Canal in 1765 goods were transported from Chorlton to Manchester via the local town of Stretford. Bricks were manufactured in the township for export, and market gardeners cultivated potatoes, cabbages and other vegetables for sale in the city markets.

Towards the end of the century, Chorlton began to develop into a more distinct suburb of the industrialised metropolis of Manchester. Factory owners and businesspeople moved out to the township's leafy streets to escape the dirt and noise of the textile mills and factories. They built attractive red-brick villas with walled gardens, on tree-lined avenues. There were hotels and public houses and later, rows of shops to serve the thriving community's needs. City workers travelled into Manchester by the omnibus service or twice-daily packet boats on the canal. Chorlton railway station opened in 1880, making it a desirable neighbourhood for commuters. Living in the vicinity of the junction of West Point were accountants, magistrates, merchants and manufacturers of textiles, metals and chemicals. Crime was low, compared to the dangerous streets of the city centre, making it: 'one of the most respectable suburbs of Manchester...covered by villa residences of some considerable pretension' (*Manchester Courier*, 27 November 1876).

On New Year's Day 1876, PC Cock took up his position at Chorlton police station. His superior officer was Superintendent Bent. James Bent was 48 years old and had joined the Lancashire Constabulary almost 30 years earlier. Born in Eccles, Salford in 1828, his father had been a member of the city's 'Old Watch', which was later replaced by Sir Robert Peel's professional new police force. Night watchmen were first appointed in 1285 to guard their local area by patrolling the streets after dark, with a lantern and a cutlass. In the seventeenth century, during the reign of Charles II, they became known as 'Charlies' and worked alongside the parish constable. Due to the low pay night watchmen were usually old and weak, as opportunities for the elderly and frail were limited. They were ridiculed by the general public and, by the nineteenth century, their duties were reduced to 'crying the hours' throughout the night.

In his memoirs, Bent recalled his father wearing a low crowned hat with a yellow band. Although the watchmen had no official uniform, Bent remembered numbers being painted on his father's coat each night with ochre. Bent's father told him a story about explaining to a newly-engaged colleague on the watch that all he had to do was to call out the hours: 'You will be at one side of the canal, and I shall be at the other, and when you hear me call the hour all you have to do is to call the same as me.' At the required time, Bent senior called out, 'Past ten o'clock, and a fine moonlight night,' to which his colleague replied, 'Same here.'

James Bent began working in a silk mill at just seven years old. Prior to the Factory Acts, young children were treated harshly and endured severe punishment at the hands of the 'overlooker' (supervisor). Bent was beaten many times with a leather strap and sustained thick welts on his arms. On 7 November 1848, just before his twenty-first birthday, Bent joined the Lancashire Constabulary. His police record describes him as 5 feet 8 inches tall, with a fair complexion, grey eyes and sandy hair. He was married with two children when he began his career in Preston as a recruit, after which he was sent to the headquarters of the Manchester Division at Pendleton. He was transferred several times and promoted through the ranks, reaching superintendent in 1868, by which time he was stationed at Old Trafford police station, commanding the division. Now with a growing family, the Bents had settled in nearby Stretford.

The *Lancashire Constabulary Journal* described Super-intendent Bent as, 'a very skilful policeman, leader and humanist'. Throughout his early career, he investigated many different types of crime, including theft, burglary, illegal gaming, assault and murder. During the year of his promotion to superintendent, he tackled an intriguing case of attempted murder by a hawker of blacking known as Travis, in Newton Heath. The itinerant salesman's wife was an inmate of Prestwich Lunatic Asylum. During a visit, Travis had taken her some Eccles cakes and, shortly after he left, his wife and another inmate began to eat them. They soon discovered that inside each cake was a dozen pins twisted into the shape of fish hooks. Superintendent Bent had the cakes analysed and found that, in addition to the pins, they contained antimony, a lead-based poison. Bent also discovered that Travis had pledged himself to another woman in the event of his wife's death, and was attempting to murder her so that he would be free to re-marry. The lovelorn salesman was sentenced to 20 years' penal servitude. Superintendent Bent kept the pins as souvenirs, handing them out to crime enthusiasts. He came under so much pressure to distribute these macabre relics that he admitted to buying 50 more pins to satisfy the public's curiosity. The year before PC Cock's death, Superintendent Bent was recognised for 25 years of 'faithful and valued services' by the local magistrates, who presented him with a silver tea service and a purse containing £75 (worth about £6,000 today).

After PC Cock's death, Superintendent Bent and his colleagues proceeded at once to the home of his prime suspects. Travelling in a cab with Inspector Whitlam, who happened to be his son-in-law, Bent stopped 150 yards away from the nursery gardens belonging to a man named Francis Deakin. Deakin's employees, John, Frank and William Habron, aged 24, 22 and 18 respectively, were staying in an outhouse where they worked as gardeners. Bent instructed his men to surround the small, brick building while he roused Francis Deakin, who was sleeping in the adjoining property of Firs Farm. One of Bent's sergeants spotted a light in the outhouse as they approached, but by the time they neared the building, it had been extinguished.

Superintendent Bent woke Deakin and informed him of Cock's murder. According to Bent, the employer responded by saying, 'Oh, dear me. I told them to let it drop, and have no more bother about it.' The superintendent had deliberately omitted to mention to Deakin that he suspected the Habron brothers of the crime. Deakin went on to exclaim, 'Oh, my God, if it is any of these men it is that young one (meaning William Habron), as he has the most abominable temper of any man I ever knew in my life.'

The senior police officer asked Deakin to accompany him to the outhouse so that when he called his men, the brothers would not take fright and abscond. After some hesitation he agreed. Francis Deakin knocked at the door and shook the latch, calling out, 'Jack! Is Jack in?' referring to John Habron. There was no answer, even though the bed they all shared was close to the entrance. He knocked a second time, but was met once again with silence. The third time he knocked, Deakin called out, 'Superintendent Bent wants to see you.' The market gardener then slipped away as fast as he could.

The outhouse was still in darkness as the lock turned and the door opened allowing Bent and his colleagues to rush into the building. It was pitch black inside, so Bent used his police lantern to peer around the room. The three young men were all in bed, the one who had opened the door having jumped back in. Bent and his men grabbed them, only to discover that they were naked, so he asked the brothers to get up and dress. Some of the clothing they had worn that day lay strewn on the bed and the floor. Bent examined each item of clothing as the brothers put them back on. He and his officers also made a cursory search of the premises.

There was a half-burned candle in an old candlestick near the fireplace, which Bent observed, 'it was much softer than I should have expected to have found if it had not recently burned.' The fire was cold and there were no other obvious sources of light. No firearms were found. As soon as the men were dressed, Superintendent Bent handcuffed them, warning, 'You three men are charged on suspicion of having killed and murdered Police Constable Cock.' The eldest brother, John, put up his hands, as high as he could while restricted by the cuffs, and replied, 'I was in bed at the time'. Frank and William Habron hung their heads down, 'appearing very nervous'.

Bent instructed the prisoners to be taken in a cab to Old Trafford police station for questioning. Before they left, he asked each one to hand over their boots so that he could inspect them. All the boots were wet, but only William's were muddy, so Superintendent Bent gave John and Frank theirs back, but retained their brother's. William then put on a spare pair. As the day dawned, the police undertook a search for the murder weapon in the gardens nearby, as well as the fields, ditches and ponds in the locality, but found nothing.

After the Habrons' arrest, Bent returned to West Point, where he remained until daylight, examining the crime scene. A private road, known as Firs Lane, ran from the junction of West Point, between Northleigh House, owned by lead merchant Samuel Gratrix, and Orleton House. There were also two gravel footpaths, which were less than 200 feet from West

Point, leading from Firs Lane into Chorlton. One ran from Firs Farm through the corn fields and was crossed by two water courses, one of which was originally known as Black Brook. Several bridges provided crossing points over the water, which was wide and deep, with very black mud. The bridges were accessed by gates, one over six feet high with spikes on the top. The second footpath contained a night soil tip and manure, with dirty water running through it.

At the entrance to Firs Lane, near the spot where PC Cock was shot, Superintendent Bent found several sets of footprints on the gravel pathway, some on Firs Lane and others on a gate stump about a yard away; they were all within ten yards of the crime scene. There were about 20 more prints on the Seymour Grove side of the junction, but they were less distinct. The prints seemed to come from at least two different pairs of boots. The dry ground was covered with sand and cinders, which made it difficult for the police officer to make impressions for comparison. Finding one footprint, which he believed had been made by one of William Habron's boots, Bent sent to the police station for them. While he waited, he placed his constables on guard to prevent onlookers from disturbing them. It began to rain so Bent covered the prints with a cardboard box.

By 1876, the analysis of footprints by the police in important cases was quite well established. Developing crime scene investigation techniques included photographing footprints and making casts with plaster of Paris, when possible. In the Road Hill House murder in 1860, when Detective Inspector Jonathan Whicher investigated the death of 3-year-old Samuel Kent, the prints of large hobnailed boots in the drawing room were important clues.

When the Habrons' boots arrived at West Point, Bent compared them with the prints to see if any of the marks tallied, with the assistance of a professional draughtsman, who confirmed that the footprints were similar. The boot impressions in the road were not clear enough to interpret. A sudden downpour of torrential rain rendered further analysis impossible. As noted in the *Manchester Times*: 'This comparison alone, however, would not have justified the police in making the arrests but for certain other matters which came to their knowledge.'

PC Cock had crossed the path of the Habron brothers several times. His intervention had resulted in two of them being summoned to court for drunk and disorderly behaviour only a week before his death. William and John appeared before the magistrate at the Manchester City Police Court charged with being drunk in Chorlton on Saturday 15 July. William was fined five shillings and costs, whilst the case against his brother was adjourned to Tuesday 1 August.

On the day of John Habron's trial at the petty sessions, Superintendent Bent received a visit in his private office from a gentleman, who remained unnamed in his memoirs but could have been Francis Deakin. The man had been at the previous court hearing and he informed Bent that he believed PC Cock to have been mistaken in the identity of John Habron. He asked the senior officer if he would withdraw the charges. When the superintendent called Cock into his office for questioning, he said, 'I am not mistaken, Mr Bent, and the gentleman knows it. He came to me when I had my arms round them, and asked me to let them go, and he would give me their names, which he did.' Satisfied with his colleague's response, Superintendent Bent insisted that the case went ahead. Shortly after, PC Cock returned to Bent's office and said, 'Mr Bent, I know these men very well. They have threatened several times to shoot me within the last few months, if I ever summoned them.'

Believing it to be an empty threat, as such expressions were 'frequently used to policemen by persons whom they had occasion to arrest', Bent responded, 'Well, Cock, you are not afraid.' The young policeman replied, 'No, I am not afraid; but I thought I would tell you what they have said.'

John Habron was discharged from court after the magistrate decided to give him the benefit of the doubt, it being his second appearance on the charge. According to Superintendent Bent, PC Cock came to him again later that day, saying, 'John Habron has just told me that he will shoot me before twelve o'clock to-night.' Bent recalled in his memoirs that Cock, despite asserting that he was not afraid, 'nevertheless seemed a little troubled in his mind.' Although this conversation was never reported in the press, Bent steadfastly maintained that the Habron brothers were the perpetrators.

After comparing the boot prints at West Point, Superintendent Bent returned to the police station, where he searched William Habron's pockets. In William's left waistcoat pocket, he found two percussion caps, which were small metal cylinders placed in the rear of a gun barrel to enable it to ignite in any weather. When asked about the caps, the labourer claimed that he knew nothing about them. Half an hour later, he changed his mind: 'Oh! Those caps that you found might have been in this pocket when Mr Deakin gave me the waistcoat some time ago.' He then told Bent that he had not been in court on the previous day when his brother was tried for drunkenness, and, in fact, he had not left Chorlton at all. Later, he had had two glasses of ale at the Royal Oak public house, and then gone to Lloyd's Hotel with John after the trial, and they were both in bed by half-past nine. Then he said, 'Stop a bit. I went to the Oak a little after nine o'clock, and bought half-an-ounce of tobacco.' He stated that his other brother, Frank, was in bed already when they returned home.

Next, Superintendent Bent questioned Frank Habron, who corroborated his brother's statement: 'Mr Bent, I know nothing about this; I was in bed at nine o'clock, and had been asleep a good while when William and John came.' John Habron also gave his version of events: 'I did go into the Lloyd's to see if William would come home; he came with me at once. We had no drink...We were in bed by half-past nine o'clock.'

Later that afternoon, Bent went once again to West Point in the company of Colonel Robert Bruce, Chief Constable of the Lancashire Constabulary. This time he found a bullet mark in the garden wall near to where PC Cock fell. He removed the brick, which was about six feet high. As Cock was just under 5 feet 8 inches tall, Bent surmised that the mark was made by the first bullet, which had missed the police officer.

The *Manchester Courier* later reported that PC Cock had spotted someone standing by Samuel Gratrix's garden wall, on the corner of Seymour Grove, at West Point. The journalist assumed that the police officer had walked over to the person, from the middle of the road, perhaps to see if he required any assistance. Then, observing that the place was 'especially favourable to his designs', the man shot PC Cock as soon as his companions were out of sight. The police believed that Cock's attacker had fled along the private road running alongside Mr Gratrix's house, and then crossed the fields back in the direction of Chorlton-cum-Hardy.

Later that day, Dr John Dill and Mr R. C. Wade, a local surgeon, carried out the post-mortem on Nicholas Cock's body at Old Trafford Station mortuary. They concluded that his death had been caused by a gunshot wound close to his right nipple. The bullet, which was rifled, had been fired from a revolver 'of first class make'. Rifling consists of cutting grooves in a spiral down the barrel of a firearm, in order to spin the bullet as it passes through to improve accuracy. The bullet had hit the police officer's fourth rib and shattered the bone, fragments of which were forced into his right lung. It had then lodged in his spinal column. The injury had caused extensive haemorrhaging. The only other external injury was a slight bruising of the face, as if PC Cock's head had come into contact with a hard surface, but the doctors dismissed this as irrelevant.

So far, all the police had to go on was the bullet removed from PC Cock's body, the indistinct boot prints found at the crime scene and the percussion caps found in William Habron's pocket. The formal proceedings were set to begin the following day.

Chapter 3

THE MOST PERFECT FOOTPRINT

"'No doubt it appeared to you to be a mere
trampled line of slush, but to my trained eyes
every mark upon its surface had a meaning.'"

(A Study in Scarlet, Sir Arthur Conan Doyle, 1887)

Since 1194, coroners have investigated sudden, unnatural or
unexplained deaths in Great Britain. Although the coroner's
role has changed over the centuries, they are still responsible
for examining cases of suspicious death. In the nineteenth
century, coroners' inquests were usually held at local public
houses, usually in a back room or upstairs, as they were often the
only building with enough space. Today a coroner is appointed
to review a death, yet in the past they were required to screen
all deaths and to adjudicate on which cases needed further
scrutiny. The coroner's inquest often ran concurrently with the
police investigation and judicial process, with solicitors, police
officers and witnesses attending both.

The inquest into Nicholas Cock's death opened at the
Northumberland Arms public house in Old Trafford on 3
August. Built on the site of a former pleasure garden, the pub
was on one of the main routes from the city centre, close to
the Pomona Docks which served the Manchester Ship Canal. It
was a squat, rather unprepossessing building with large rooms,

likely to have been used for auctions and public meetings as well as inquests.

The county coroner, Frederick Price, opened the inquest, which was attended by the chief constable, as well as the prosecuting solicitor. The coroner began by stating his intention to take evidence of the victim's identity and of the post-mortem examination report only. Superintendent Bent was the first witness. He confirmed that the deceased was PC Nicholas Cock, who was 'not quite 22 years of age' and had been stationed at Chorlton-cum-Hardy. He described how he had witnessed Cock die at 1.10 am on the morning of 2 August at the home of Dr Dill.

The next to testify, Dr John Dill, recounted how two police officers had brought the injured officer to his house at Gordon Villa on Upper Chorlton Road, at 12.30 am. They were still accompanied by the young man PC Cock had spoken to just before the shooting, John Massey Simpson. On examining Cock, Dr Dill discovered that he had sustained a gunshot wound to the right breast. Later that day, he had performed the post-mortem.

Post-mortem examinations for medico-legal purposes were still developing throughout the nineteenth century, as pathologists and physicians published new procedures and techniques. Towards the end of the century, standard practices were refined and adopted. Post-mortems had to be always undertaken in daylight, rather than at night, as was often the case. First the clothes were removed from the body, and physical features and distinguishing marks noted, before the examination commenced. A thorough external examination was then carried out, including the measurement and assessment of external injuries, such as indications of strangulation or stab wounds. This was followed by an internal examination, during which all the body's cavities were opened, and organs and tissue removed for further analysis.

Dr Dill carried out PC Cock's post-mortem with his colleague, Mr Wade. At the inquest, he described the procedure in detail: 'On opening the chest, I was able to trace the course of the bullet through the right lung, and found it lodged in the internal part of the spine.' He held up the bullet to show the jury.

The doctor then described Nicholas Cock's general health. His organs were 'quite healthy' although his liver was slightly enlarged. The skull was intact and had not been fractured, despite bruising on the face which may have been sustained during his fall. His brain showed 'signs of incipient disease', which the doctor did not explain, but it was 'free from congestion' (swelling). Dr Dill concluded: 'The deceased was a fine, strong man...I do not think that the effects of the bruise at the side of the head, or the condition of the liver, or brain, had anything to do with causing his death.' The inquest was adjourned to the following Wednesday, to allow time for Chief Constable Bruce to collate the evidence.

Despite its proximity to lawless inner city Manchester, which had one of the highest crime rates in the country, the township of Chorlton-cum-Hardy was a peaceful and generally trouble-free place. Occasionally there were burglaries and robberies, especially at the wealthy residences in the area, but many of the criminal activities were rural in nature. There were bouts of poaching and theft of farm animals and products, possibly due to unemployment, and sometimes perpetrated by gangs of thieves from other areas. There was also a high incidence of alcohol-related offences, such as drunkenness, brawling and illegal prizefighting.

Serious crimes like murder were rare, although earlier in the century there had been a number of infanticides in the district, mostly committed by desperate mothers, many of whom were unmarried domestic servants, trying to rid themselves of the burden of an illegitimate child. Only two high profile murders had taken place in Chorlton before that of Nicholas Cock, both occurring several decades before his death.

In 1838, Mary Moore lived with her husband Joseph, on Chorlton Green, in the heart of the township. Forty-nine-year-old Mary worked at the nearby Dog House Farm, where one of her duties was to take vegetables and fruit from the farm for sale at Smithfield Market, in central Manchester. On 19 June 1838, Mary set out for the market at 6.30 am, in the company of labourer Thomas Hooley, who drove the farm cart. She had a successful morning at the market, selling her produce, mostly gooseberries, and had arranged to meet Thomas at 11 am for a ride back to Chorlton. When Mary failed to turn up on time, the cart driver made his way home alone. A little later Mary walked back to the farm, meeting a local farmer en route. They travelled together for a while, chatting, and parted company on the road at 2 pm, about ten minutes away from Dog House Farm. She never reached her destination.

The following day Mary's brother-in-law and one of her co-workers mounted a search in the local area. At about 8 pm, they found her body lying in a ditch, in a field lane near the farm entrance. Her market takings, bag and umbrella were missing, although her purse was still there, with some money inside. Mary had died from two heavy blows to the head and it was later assumed that she had been killed elsewhere and dragged into the ditch.

Initially four labourers, who had apparently been looking for work around Chorlton, were arrested but the charges were soon dropped after witnesses testified to their being in central Manchester excavating a tunnel on the canal. Later, 25-year-old former marine William Hodge was charged with her murder. Witnesses had seen Hodge attempting to conceal a parcel in the hedge, near where Mary was found. He also had a scrap of paper similar to the paper Mary had wrapped her takings in. William Hodge was tried at the Liverpool Assizes in August 1839 and acquitted due to lack of evidence. Mary Moore's killer was never found.

Almost a decade later, another incident with a fatal outcome took place in Chorlton and this murder had an uncanny link to the present case. In May 1847, market gardener Francis Deakin was drinking in a beerhouse with his friends George Leach and John Cookson, perhaps celebrating the recent birth of his sixth child. An afternoon of beer and rum led to an argument between George Leach and his wife, who owned the beerhouse. When George started to hurl insults at her, Francis stepped in to defend Mrs Leach. Enraged, George ran into the kitchen and grabbed a carving knife, meeting Francis in the passage. Shouting, 'I'll have no man interfering with me and my wife,' he lunged at Francis and stabbed him. George was immediately sorry for what he had done and expressed the desperate hope that he had not killed his friend, but Francis Deakin died from his wounds. George Leach was convicted of aggravated manslaughter and transported for life.

Francis's wife, Martha, was left alone with six children, ranging from 15 years to a few days old. Helped by her family, she took over the management of their market garden business and supported her children until her death, 11 years later at the age of 46. By this time, her eldest son, William, was already married with a young son, so the younger members of the Deakin family were left in the care of 16-year-old Francis junior, who looked after his brother and two sisters, whilst assuming responsibility for the market garden. Francis married in 1864 and had one son before his wife died. By the mid-1870s, he had become a prosperous nurseryman and was re-married with three more children. He lived at Firs Farm, where he employed the three Habron brothers, together with at least five more workers.

Born in Ireland in the 1850s, the Habrons arrived in England towards the end of the following decade, in search of work. Irish migration to the mainland had mostly begun during the Industrial Revolution, reaching a peak in the late 1840s, during the Great Famine of 1846-1851. Successive bouts of potato blight ravaged the crops and, in the absence of intervention by the British government, led to starvation and disease, causing the deaths of about a million people, almost an eighth of the population. Two million others emigrated to escape the disaster. Life for the Habron brothers began in the devastation of the famine and, as soon as they were old enough, they left their homeland for a better life in England.

The Habrons docked at Liverpool and then travelled to Manchester, where they settled in Chorlton. The eldest brother, Thomas, went into the employ of John Gresley, who owned a market garden near Lloyd's Hotel. In 1871, at the age of 29, Thomas had already been widowed and had a five-year-old son. Meanwhile, John, Francis and William Habron were engaged by Francis Deakin who, perhaps because of his own precarious childhood, was more sympathetic to struggling families. *Lloyd's Weekly Newspaper* reported that: 'They bore excellent characters on the whole, and regularly remitted a portion of their wages to old folks at home.' Apart from a previous summons for drunkenness, a year before PC Cock's murder, their reputation was generally positive.

Following the inquest into Nicholas Cock's death, on Thursday 3 August, the three Habron brothers appeared before the magistrates at the Manchester County Police Court, at Strangeways. The bench was chaired by Sir John Iles Mantell. The solicitor Thomas Henry Crofton stood for the prosecution, and William Cobbett for the prisoners' defence, which would have been paid for by the Habron family as there was no legal aid at the time. Also present in the forbidding Gothic-style court was the Deputy Chief Constable of Lancashire Constabulary, Captain Legge. According to the *Manchester Courier*, 'The court was crowded and great excitement was manifested in the case.'

Defence and prosecution agreed on an adjournment until the following Monday, after the coroner's inquest, which was due to take place on the Wednesday, as 'it was desirable that the two inquiries should not clash.' Sir Mantell agreed to the adjournment and ordered the prisoners to be remanded in custody. They were then removed from the dock. The police now had a few days during which to prove their suspicions correct. The investigation was led by Superintendent Bent who, although he was not officially recognised as a detective – as the CID was still in its infancy – nevertheless engaged in what we would regard as 'detective' duties: 'From the very commencement of my career in this police force I was constantly employed as a detective,' he asserted in his memoirs.

Bent regularly undertook surveillance duties in plain clothes, usually at race meetings, 'with the object of detecting pickpockets and gamblers'. He even taught himself how to operate gaming instruments to learn the tricks gamblers used to cheat their players so that he could more effectively expose their various scams and ruses. At a carnival in Eccles, Bent arrested a man with a wooden arm running a gaming table, but could only find a small amount of cash on him. A while later, it occurred to the detective that the man might have concealed his winnings in his artificial limb. When he examined the arm, he discovered that a socket had been hollowed in the elbow to hide the stash.

At race meetings, Superintendent Bent would lie on the grass and peer through the crowds, watching out for any suspicious-looking racegoers. He was once working undercover at the Old Trafford Race Ground, when he spotted a man entering the Trafford Arms Hotel. As followed the suspect into the scullery, the man saw him and turned back. Pretending to wash his hands, Bent waited in the scullery until the suspect reappeared. In full view of the disguised officer, the man stole a half leg of mutton, and even asked him for a knife, in exchange for a share in his spoils. Superintendent Bent arrested the thief and found several pies in his pocket. Later the prisoner confided in Bent that he had mistaken him for an old cabdriver. Bent concluded: 'I have no doubt my dress deceived him.'

It was quite common for Victorian detectives to don disguises, which was especially effective in an era when one's dress denoted one's occupation and social standing. When Bent was instructed to investigate the alleged theft of several bales of rags from a wharf, he undertook surveillance of his suspect, who was a hawker with a barrow. Soon discovering the hawker's mother's address, he went to question her at her home. In order not to alarm the elderly woman, he dressed as a clergyman, with a white 'choker', a shabby coat and an old hat. He even procured some religious tracts. Bent engaged the suspect's mother in conversation on her doorstep and learned the whereabouts of her son, whom he later arrested.

On another occasion, Bent concealed his identity whilst visiting a pawnbroker's by covering his face with a handkerchief and 'pretending to have the tic'. At other times, he blackened his face with mud, disarranged his clothing by unbuttoning his coat and behaved as though he was drunk. When he brought a housebreaker to justice whilst in disguise as a labourer, the magistrate commended him saying that he was 'one of the best detective officers the county had ever produced' and that if Bent were on the beat in his own neighbourhood, he would feel as safe 'as if it were guarded by a regiment of soldiers'.

Superintendent Bent developed many clever techniques to solve crimes, including marking money to detect theft. On night duty, when he was passing detached houses, he would place a stick or a stone between the gates. Then, when he walked past again, he would check to see if it had been disturbed. He once tied a piece of fine weaver's silk from a bobbin across the door of a known poacher and when the man left the house in the middle of the night, Bent followed the thread's trail.

In addition to his practical sleuthing skills, Superintendent James Bent had an unerring instinct for wrongdoing, as he expressed in his favourite adage, 'Always believe everybody guilty until you prove them innocent.' He would apply it with vigour and determination in the case of the Habron brothers.

The first concrete piece of evidence in the case was the bullet retrieved from PC Cock's spine. Expert gunsmith William Griffiths, who owned a shop on Bridge Street in central Manchester, concluded that it was part of a copper cartridge fired from a .442 revolver. The .442 Webley firearm was introduced in 1868 and was commonly used by the Royal Irish Constabulary. Available in the UK until the 1950s, it was popular on the streets as a weapon for self-defence. However, as the firearm used to kill PC Cock had not been found, it was impossible to link the bullet to the perpetrator, so Superintendent Bent focused on the footprints he had found near the crime scene.

Identification of suspects through footprints has been used in criminal investigations since the early nineteenth century. Marks made at a crime scene by footwear can link a suspect to the scene, as well as providing vital intelligence about the incident, such as the position and movement of individuals. The first detective to use footprinting was the French ex-convict and police informer, Eugène Vidocq, who established the world's first detective department, the Brigade de la Sûreté (Security Bureau) in Paris, in 1812. Vidocq pioneered many investigative techniques, such as record-keeping and mugshots, as well as the examination of footprints. He used this technique successfully in the apprehension of a former police agent, who was implicated in the theft of a large quantity of lead from a house under construction, by matching the agent's boots with prints in the soil at the building site. The master detective was also the first to use plaster of Paris to make casts of footprints.

Throughout the Victorian era, footprints were vital evidence in crime scene investigation, especially as shoes and boots were not usually custom-made and therefore, unique. By the 1880s, the police were using plaster of Paris to preserve shoe and boot prints. Another Frenchman, physician and criminologist Alexandre Lacassagne, perfected the technique and was even able to make casts in the snow by using salt to form an icy layer around the impression. He also developed an instrument called a pantograph, which duplicated prints to scale, through a framework of parallelograms.

In Britain, William Augustus Guy, professor of forensic medicine at King's College London, published *The Principles of Forensic Science* in 1844. Subsequent editions contained information about footprinting. He recommended heating footprints with a hot iron and dusting them with powdered stearic acid to preserve them, a method recommended by the French chemist, F. Hugoulin. Guy stressed the importance of impressions left by footwear, as the position and shape of patches or nails could yield the first link in the chain of evidence.

By the time the final edition of Guy's work was published in 1888, Sir Arthur Conan Doyle had adopted the practices for his fictional sleuth. In the first ever Sherlock Holmes story, 'A Study in Scarlet', which appeared in 1887, the detective extolls the virtues of footprinting: 'There is no branch of detective science which is so important and so much neglected as the art of tracing footsteps. Happily, I have always laid great stress upon it.' So did Superintendent James Bent.

Superintendent Bent found 'the most perfect footprint' very close to where PC Cock was shot, in the road two or three yards away from the gate of Samuel Gratrix's house. Believing that it had been made by William Habron's left boot, he compared it with the mark left in the cinders on the path. The outer row of nails on William's boot was so worn down that it was difficult to count the number of nails. However, the inner row, comprising 13 nails, corresponded exactly to the number visible in the impression. Furthermore, the nails in the middle of the sole, near the toe and on the heel all corresponded with the print.

When Bent made a new impression with the boot next to the original print, it confirmed his opinion that the footprint found near the scene of the murder was made by William Habron's left boot. Together with the percussion caps discovered in William's waistcoat pocket, the footprint put the 18-year-old labourer firmly in the frame for murder.

Chapter 4

A MYSTERIOUS MAN

'Take nothing on its looks; take everything on
evidence. There's no better rule.'

(Great Expectations, Charles Dickens, 1861)

Constable Nicholas Cock was the tenth police officer in the
Lancashire Constabulary to lose his life in the line of duty. The
first, Special Constable Joseph Halstead, was beaten to death
with an iron railing taken from a church, during rioting in
Colne in 1840. The unrest had erupted during a protest against
the establishment of the newly-appointed rural police. Three
men were charged with Halstead's murder, but only one was
convicted and sentenced to death.

There were no further police deaths in the county for almost
two decades, until PC Matthew Sharp drowned in the canal at
St Helens, whilst on night duty in 1858. Ten years later, another
constable died in the same way, but this time in Wigan. Of the
remaining deaths, one officer was shot dead, another trampled
by a horse at Manchester Races, while three more died of head
injuries sustained during disturbances. In 1869, Constable
John Parker died from hydrophobia after being bitten by a
rabid dog in Rochdale. PC Cock was the first officer to suffer
fatal injuries in the township of Chorlton-cum-Hardy.

~~~

26

On Saturday 5 August 1876, Nicholas Cock was laid to rest in the churchyard of St Clement's, which he had often passed on his beat. The funeral cortège left Old Trafford police station just before 3 pm and processed through the streets to the church. More than a hundred officers accompanied their fallen colleague, led by the Manchester City Police Band, as well as various divisions of the Lancashire Constabulary under the command of Superintendent Bent. Also in attendance were local magistrates, including the chair of the bench, and the solicitors involved in the case.

The only relative present at the funeral was PC Cock's sister, who was living in Durham. Most of Nicholas's surviving siblings had remained in Cornwall, perhaps due to travel costs – although travel by train was quicker and cheaper than by road, it would have been very expensive to cover such a great distance. Two of his sisters were married and the youngest, Mary Ann, had stayed at home to care for their mother. Married with nine children, his eldest brother James had followed their father down their mines, while John had joined the Royal Navy. After his first wife's death, the third surviving brother Reuben had emigrated to Australia, where he had soon married again.

St Clement's Church was built in 1779 on Chorlton Green, where there had been a chapel since 1512. A modest red brick building with a tower, aisles were added in 1837 and two years later it was designated a parish church due to the growing population. By the 1860s, the church had fallen into disrepair due to a lack of funds, and local landowner Lord Egerton donated some land for a new church, which was opened in 1866. However, the parishioners remained opposed to the new building and continued to attend the original church until its demolition in 1940.

As PC Cock's cortège steadily made its way to St Clement's, thousands of people lined the route. Described in the press as a 'cold-blooded murder', the shocked residents of Victorian Manchester were keen to pay their respects and both the church, which seated 420, and the graveyard were packed full of mourners. Reverend John Edmund Booth delivered the service, reported as 'of unusually impressive character'. At the end of the solemn ceremony the minister gave a brief address at the graveside, in which he urged PC Cock's colleagues 'not to let such an occurrence, shocking though it was, deter them from the faithful discharge of duty.'

Two days after Constable Cock's funeral, the three Habron brothers appeared again before the magistrates, at the Manchester County Police Court in Strangeways. After stating their respective ages, they were charged formally with the wilful murder of PC Nicholas Cock. Solicitor for the prosecution, Thomas Henry Crofton, proposed a further adjournment to Friday, after the inquest. Midday on Friday 11 August was agreed upon and the prisoners were held on remand for the rest of the week. In the meantime, the adjourned inquest took place, during which the witnesses were examined in public for the first time.

On Wednesday 9 August, the adjourned inquest opened at the Northumberland Arms. The Chief Constable of the Lancashire county police, Colonel Bruce, was present, along with the respective solicitors. The first witness to take the stand was law student John Massey Simpson, who had chatted to PC Cock on the night of his death, and had been one of the first people to come to the officer's aid after the shooting. He recounted the events of the night of 1 August.

John Simpson had spent the evening at a friend's house in Chorlton-cum-Hardy, and had left about 11.40 pm, returning home along Chorlton Lane. At Reigate Farm he passed PC Cock, who was standing on the footpath. He bid the officer goodnight and walked on. A few minutes later, Cock overtook him and they continued together towards the junction of West Point. When they arrived at the boundary of PC Cock's beat, another officer, PC James Beanland, joined them and the three men chatted for a few minutes, after which John Simpson continued his journey home alone. In court, Simpson stated that during the conversation with the two officers, PC Cock had told his colleague about the case he had attended in court that day relating to the Habron brothers. He commented that their employer Francis Deakin 'must have thought very well of the men, as he had been instrumental in obtaining legal assistance'. Simpson added that PC Cock, 'seemed to imply that the case was not finished; that something further would arise.' The law student had left PC Cock standing at the junction, next to a large house.

Mr Crofton asked Simpson whether he had noticed any other individuals in the vicinity and he replied that he had spotted a man passing directly under the gas lamp at the corner of Upper Chorlton Road and Seymour Grove. The man had 'walked in a peculiar manner, as if he had not made up his mind which way to go'. He turned on to the left-hand side of Seymour Grove and disappeared under some trees overhanging the footpath. Under further questioning, the witness agreed that the side of the road on which the man passed was less frequented than the other. He gave a detailed description of the anonymous figure: 'He wore a short coat, jacket shape and brown in colour. He also had a "pot" (bowler) hat on.' As he passed the three men at the junction, Simpson noticed him looking in their direction for a moment, before walking on. The two officers also saw him but said nothing.

Simpson then gave an account of the events that took place after he had left the junction. He had walked about 150 or 160 yards down Upper Chorlton Road, towards his home, when he heard a shot from a firearm, coming from behind him, at West Point. A second later, he heard another: 'The reports were sharp as if proceeding from a revolver.' As he turned back, he saw Constable Beanland in the middle of the road blowing his whistle and Constable Cock on the footpath, having fallen more or less in the same spot where he had left him. Simpson ran back and bent down to the injured officer, as Beanland tried to raise him from the ground. Another passerby came over, William West, as well as the two night soil men, who arrived with their foul-smelling carts, after transporting the city's human waste.

Simpson unfastened Cock's tunic and shirt. By the light of a lantern, he noticed a slight bruise on the right side of the officer's head, above his cheekbone. He placed his hand on Cock's chest, near his heart, and found blood flowing from a wound in his right breast. Together with the others, he placed PC Cock into one of the carts. Two more officers arrived and they all travelled with Cock to Dr Dill's surgery, where Simpson watched him die.

In court, Simpson recalled PC Cock saying, 'Let me alone, you are killing me', as they were trying to place him into the cart. At Dr Dill's surgery, Simpson said that Cock seemed to recover a little, after the doctor had laid him on the sofa and administered some water and brandy. Sergeant Thompson, one of the officers who came to PC Beanland's aid, had asked him several times, 'Who shot you?' According to Simpson, Cock had replied, 'Leave me alone, and I'll tell you', yet he did not make a formal statement. Sergeant Thompson questioned him further but by this time PC Cock was struggling to breathe, and replied, 'I don't know; you are killing me.'

The following morning, John Simpson went to Old Trafford police station to identify the man he had seen under the gaslight. He went into a room with Superintendent Bent and the suspect was instructed to walk across the floor in front of him. Simpson told the court that he had not seen the man's face clearly enough to recognise him, but he was wearing clothes that resembled those of the stranger, and he appeared to have been about the same height. However, he was still unsure: 'I have an impression that the man I saw on the night of the murder was older-looking than the one I saw in Superintendent Bent's presence.' The foreman of the jury then asked Simpson if the man under the lamp had walked in a crouching position or upright. Simpson replied that 'he seemed to stoop somewhat... He walked in a faltering, loose kind of way, apparently not knowing where he was going.' When questioned further, the witness was not able to say whether the suspect at the police station had an upright posture. He simply said, 'I did not notice sufficiently.' The suspect was William Habron.

The next witness to testify about the night PC Cock was killed was PC James Beanland. Beanland had been on duty in Seymour Grove and Upper Chorlton Road. About midnight, he was walking from Chorlton to West Point, when he met his colleague and James Simpson. At 12.07 am Simpson left them and a minute or two later, PC Beanland saw a man coming down Upper Chorlton Road towards the junction, opposite where he was standing with PC Cock. The man crossed the road and turned the corner into Seymour Grove. As he passed by the gas lamp, Beanland said to Cock, 'Who is that man?' to which he replied, 'I don't know.'

PC Beanland told his colleague to stay there while he went to find out what the man was up to. Carrying his lantern, he followed the direction the man had taken to the house of Samuel Gratrix on the left-hand side of Seymour Grove. Although it was a fine night, it was very dark with no moonlight and PC Beanland was unable to see the man he was following clearly. The police officer passed through the garden gate and shone his light into the window of the house. He tried the door but it was locked. All this took about a minute. As PC Beanland turned around and came back down the steps, he heard a shot, followed by a flash of light. The two night soil men were passing in their carts and they shouted out at the sound, their horses panicking. A second shot rang out and another flash. PC Beanland heard someone cry, 'Oh, murder, murder; I'm shot; I'm shot.'

The constable ran as fast as he could back to West Point, from where the direction of the shouts had come, but he could not see PC Cock as it was too dark. He turned on his lantern and found his colleague lying on his right side, moaning heavily. Beanland asked, 'Oh! Cock, whatever is the matter?' When Cock made no reply, he blew his whistle for assistance and called the cart drivers to come back. James Simpson reappeared, as well as two other police officers, and together they conveyed PC Cock to the surgery. In court, PC Beanland recalled that during the short journey in the cart, having noticed the other officers, Cock had looked up at him and said, 'Who's this?' Despite his injuries, Cock greeted Sergeant Ewan and then said, 'How do?' to Sergeant Thompson also.

In response to questions from the prosecution, PC Beanland described the man he had seen under the gas lamp on the corner. He was dressed in dark clothing, wearing what looked like a short coat. The officer could not distinguish the colour of his clothes, nor what sort of hat he was wearing. He was of medium stature, about 5 feet 8 inches tall. Unlike Simpson, Beanland had had a good view of the man's face: 'He seemed to be a young man of about 22 years of age, and he was of fresh complexion.' He said that he had walked quickly and 'in an ordinary way'. He then recalled how he had attended Habron brothers' hearing at the police court earlier in the day, and he reflected that William 'was something like the man I saw on the night of the murder.'

In the 1870s, the police had very few tools at their disposal with which to identify suspects definitively. Apart from witness statements, they had to rely on their skills of observation and memory. Investigators had to memorise or note down a suspect's details, in an attempt to link them to offences. In the police books held at the local police stations, or in their own personal casebooks, detectives recorded approximate age, height and stature, and physical characteristics, such as hair, eye colour, and complexion.

Distinguishing marks were particularly helpful for the purposes of identification, including deformities and injuries; discolouration of the hair and skin; scars and tattoos. Dress, speech and manner were also important indicators of an individual's background and status in society.

Victorian detectives made regular visits to prisons to observe the inmates. In this way, law enforcers gathered crucial information with which they could link habitual offenders to future cases. In 1871, the Prevention of Crimes Act introduced more systematic methods of tracking offenders after their release from prison, using photography to record an image of those arrested. The photographing of criminals had begun in the 1840s, soon after the invention of photography. In the late 1880s, French police officer and researcher Alphonse Bertillon developed the modern standard practice, when he introduced the method of taking two photographs of the subject: one face-on and the other in profile. He added descriptions to a file card alongside the image, creating a dossier for each individual. Bertillon also pioneered a system to identify criminals using anthropometric measurements. He devised 11 separate measurements, including the length and width of the head, their height, and the length of the left foot. All the details were entered on a card and catalogued so that the police could identify a suspect with accuracy and speed. This practice, known as 'bertillonage', was adopted by Scotland Yard in 1894.

~~~

In 1876, Superintendent Bent and his colleagues at the Lancashire Constabulary were struggling to identify their perpetrator as they only had two contradictory witness statements, from James Massey Simpson and PC James Beanland. At the inquest on 9 August, more witnesses took the stand in an attempt to piece together the events of the night of the police officer's murder.

At about midnight, on 1 August, William West was walking home up Upper Chorlton Road. He heard the two shots ahead of him and ran straight to the junction. James Simpson was running in front of him. West saw Constable Beanland, the night soil men and Simpson, all trying to help PC Cock. He did not see anyone else.

The two night soil carters, Abraham Ellison and William Morrell, were both employed by the Stretford Local Board to take human waste from the privies and cesspools in central Manchester to the suburbs, where it was used as fertiliser in nurseries and gardens. Both men were riding in Ellison's cart with the other cart fastened behind it. Before the shooting, Ellison had seen PC Cock walking on the footpath looking in the direction of Seymour Grove. The carter had driven past another ten yards when he heard the first shot. His horse reared but he managed to rein it in. Ellison stopped the cart and turned around, seeing PC Cock running back towards West Point. The police officer was about halfway across the road when he fell to the ground. Ellison heard him scream, 'Murder' three times. When PC Beanland called out to him, Ellison turned the horses round and went back to the junction. He did not see anyone else either. William Morrell corroborated his testimony.

The next witness was Constable William Ewan from the Lancashire Constabulary. He added that he had run down Seymour Grove to West Point when he heard the shots, but had not seen anyone. On the way to Dr Dill's in the cart, he asked PC Cock if he knew who had shot him. PC Cock replied, 'I don't know', but then a few seconds later he said, 'They have done me this time.' At the surgery, PC West had asked him again, to which the injured police officer answered, 'Leave me be and I'll tell you.'

Nicholas Cock died a quarter of an hour later, without revealing the identity of his killer. Superintendent James Bent described what happened next. Having received news of PC Cock's shooting at about 12.45 am, Superintendent Bent immediately proceeded in a cab to Dr Dill's surgery, after giving orders to his officers to surround the outbuilding in which the Habron brothers were living. PC Cock died ten minutes after Bent's arrival, after which he went straight to Firs Farm, arriving about 1.30 am. In court, he recounted how he had gone to Deakin's house and asked him to rouse the Habrons. Once the door was opened, Superintendent Bent rushed in, his officers flashing their lanterns in the darkened room. As the brothers were still in bed and naked, Bent insisted on examining each item of their clothing before they dressed. He commented that 'the prisoners did not appear as if they had been asleep,' and they did not ask him why he had come. Bent noted that William's boots were 'wet and muddy'.

The first clue found by the officers was the recently extinguished candle. Bent commented: 'The candle was much softer than I should have expected to have found it if not recently burned.' He handcuffed the brothers and cautioned them, noting that John claimed to have been in bed at the time, although Bent had not mentioned any time or place connected with the murder.

The superior officer then gave an account of his return to the crime scene and his ensuing examination of the footprints found on the lane near to where PC Cock was shot, 'which I believed had been made by one of the boots worn by William Habron.' After he sent to the police station for the boot, he confirmed that 'the two were alike in every way.' He then produced the percussion caps in court, explaining how he had found them in William's waistcoat pocket.

Following his statement, Superintendent Bent relayed the private conversation he had had with PC Cock on the day of his death, after John Habron's trial for drunkenness earlier that afternoon. PC Cock had complained that the brothers had threatened him: 'These are the same men who have promised to do for me.' Bent concluded, 'That was the reason why I at once went to Chorlton when I heard of the murder.'

Under cross-examination, he reiterated his conviction that the brothers were guilty: 'I suspected these three men from the first.' Presenting the footprints as evidence, he asserted, 'I have no doubt in my mind, although I have no means of showing it, that the indistinct impressions were produced by the boots of William and John Habron.'

A member of the jury, Mr Leverett, commented that there was a discrepancy between William's right and left boot, as the third row of nails on the left one, was an eighth of an inch further from the second row than on the right boot. Superintendent Bent conceded that he had not spotted the difference, and the juryman concluded: 'There is not a boot like that in Manchester today.' The police officer added that he had been unable to make any further examination of the prints at the scene as 'the rain came down in torrents and washed away the marks.' He added that there was easy access from Francis Deakin's outhouse to the path where he found the footprints.

The final witness in the inquest was local watchmaker Frederick Wilcox. He remembered cleaning John Habron's watch about three months before the murder and returning it to the labourer at his workplace. John told Wilcox about an argument he had had the previous evening with PC Cock, outside Lloyd's Hotel. Habron said that the police officer had threatened to summons him, adding, 'If that "little bobby" ever does anything to me or either of my brothers, by God, I'll shoot him!' As he spoke the words, he raised his front finger in the air. Frank had agreed with his brother's words but Frederick Wilcox took no notice at the time, as he thought it was a 'wild threat'. These words would form the basis of the ongoing investigation into the Habron brothers and their strained relationship with PC Nicholas Cock.

Chapter 5

A WILD THREAT

'But as inevitably as a great number of working-
men fall prey to drink, just so inevitably does it
manifest its ruinous influence upon the body and
mind of its victims.'

*(The Condition of the Working Class in England, Friedrich
Engels, 1845)*

In the wake of the Industrial Revolution, Manchester's
population exploded during the nineteenth century, from some
77,000 people in 1801 to 316,000 in 1851. It would double
again by the end of the century. Workers and their families
poured into the city from towns and villages in other parts of
Britain, as well as from other countries such as Italy, Ireland,
Poland and Russia, most of them fleeing poverty or religious
persecution. Inevitably, the crime rate increased too. HMP
Manchester, known as Strangeways because of its location
in Strangeways Park, opened in 1868, replacing the New
Bailey Prison. Designed by Alfred Waterhouse, with its iconic
ventilation tower and forbidding Gothic design, the institution
was modelled on Pentonville Prison and housed 1,000 inmates.
In the same year, new Manchester courtrooms were opened
next door. Their jurisdiction extended to areas outside the
cities of Manchester and Salford, which included the township

of Chorlton-cum-Hardy.

On Friday 11 August 1876, the three Habron brothers attended the police court, jointly charged with the murder of PC Nicholas Cock. On this occasion, there were five magistrates on the bench and, once again, Chief Constable Bruce was in attendance. The prosecuting solicitor, Thomas Henry Crofton, opened the proceedings with a summary of the events of the night PC Cock met his death. He mentioned the lone man seen walking in the direction of Firs Farm, who then appeared to change his mind and turn down Seymour Grove, 'all the time being underneath the trees which overhung the footpath'. He explained how PC Beanland had suspected that the stranger was intending to commit a burglary and so had followed him into Mr Gratrix's garden, only to lose sight of him seconds before the shots rang out.

Mr Crofton reminded the court how, when the police arrested the brothers, William's boots were wet and muddy, and that they subsequently matched the prints found on the footpath near to where PC Cock fell. They also discovered the percussion caps in his waistcoat pocket. Furthermore, the witnesses he proposed to call would recount threats made by the Habrons to the police officer, during the months before his death.

The first witnesses to testify were John Massey Simpson and William West, the two men who had been walking home near West Point at midnight on 1 August. They repeated the evidence they had given at the inquest two days earlier. After them came a new witness, ironmonger Donald McLennan, who worked in a shop on Oxford Road in central Manchester. He stated that on either Monday 31 July or Tuesday 1 August (he wasn't sure which date it was), between 3 pm and 4 pm, William Habron came into the ironmonger's and asked to see some cartridges. McLennan asked him what kind he wanted, but the defendant did not know. The ironmonger explained that there were two kinds in the shop window and, as he went over to the display to take some out, Habron said, 'I will go outside and point out the kind I want.' Outside the shop, he indicated that he wished to see Eley's .450 central fire cartridges, which were sold in boxes of 50. McLennan offered to sell him a box for three shillings and three pence, but Habron replied that he would only like to buy a small quantity.

When Donald McLennan explained that he was unable to break into a box of cartridges, the customer replied that he would leave them for the time being and consult someone else about it. As he was about the leave the shop, McLennan offered to show him a revolver, in order to give him a better idea of what he might be looking for. Encouraged by a positive response from Habron, McLennan loaded the gun and they discussed the price. Soon after, Habron left the shop without making a purchase. His visit lasted about five to seven minutes, and there were no other customers present, just McLennan and another assistant.

Under cross-examination, Donald McLennan admitted that he had never seen William Habron before his visit to the shop and that he had recognised him when he saw him in the dock: 'I am certain that the prisoner William Habron is the man who came into our shop.' McLennan's colleague corroborated his evidence.

After Dr Dill and Mr Wade re-stated the medical evidence, the watchmaker Frederick Wilcox told the jury about the threats he had overheard John and Frank Habron making to PC Cock. PC James Beanland deposed that he believed that the prisoner William Habron was the suspicious man he saw pass by just before the murder: 'I will not swear he is the same man, but he resembles him.' The case was adjourned to the following day.

In the nineteenth century, Manchester was the binge-drinking capital of Britain. By the mid-1800s, there were already more than 1,500 beerhouses in the city and the number increased steadily during the ensuing decades. Industry figures for 1876 reveal that an average of 34.5 gallons of beer and 1.3 gallons of spirits per person were consumed. In 1874, alcohol-related offences, such as drunkenness, disorderly behaviour, assault, and wilful damage, accounted for nearly half of the offences committed. The quiet township of Chorlton-cum-Hardy was not exempt from alcohol-fuelled crime, especially when groups of rowdy drinkers from other parts of the city visited the local hostelries. Heavy drinking often led to bouts of fighting and criminal damage. The Habron brothers were well-known for their drinking and they frequented Lloyd's Hotel and the Royal Oak public house. The Lloyd's was built in 1870, just outside the centre of Chorlton, and still exists today. The original Royal Oak building, on the road leading from Chorlton to West Point, was demolished in the 1920s, but a public house with the same name was built on the other side of the road, which remains open to this day.

On the next day of the hearing, on Saturday 12 August, the landlord of the Lloyd's Hotel, Alfred Love, testified that he had been present at West Point on 2 August, when Superintendent Bent compared the footprints on the path with William Habron's boot. A draughtsman by profession, Love confirmed that one of the boots matched the impressions exactly. A waitress at the public house, Anne Cavers, said that on the evening of Tuesday 1 August, William came into the Lloyd's with one of his brothers, at about 10 pm. The brothers were so much alike that she could not tell them apart, although she was certain one was William. They had two glasses of ale each and stayed for about half an hour. Cavers overheard one of the men saying that he had been in the police court earlier that day, but he had been 'let off'. They left Lloyd's together at 10.30 pm.

Labourer John Walsh, who worked in a local nursery garden with the fourth Habron brother Thomas, testified that he had been with William and John Habron in Lloyd's that evening. After drinking 'a small quantity of ale' they left about 9.30 pm, after which he saw the brothers walking back towards their lodgings. Earlier that evening Walsh had seen Frank Habron in his bed. According to the report in the *Manchester Weekly Times*, when Superintendent Bent asked William Habron about his whereabouts on that day, he had said that he had gone to the Royal Oak for some tobacco about 9 pm, leaving half an hour later.

Another labourer, John Hulton, remembered drinking with the Habrons in the Bowling Green pub, near Chorlton Green, the year before. When a disturbance broke out, John had bragged that if it had happened in Ireland, they would have been prepared for a fight as the Irish generally went out armed.

~~~

The police had interviewed local people, including a boy named Edward Blakeley, who was staying that same night in Firs Lane, which led to Firs Farm where the Habrons lived. He spoke of being woken by a dog barking between 11.45 pm and 12.30 am. Another witness, Mary Brundrett, also heard a noise 'as of someone running past the end of the house' about 12.30 am. The house where she lived backed onto another road leading to Firs Farm. When questioned, Brundrett admitted that it was not unusual to hear noises at that time of night. She woke her husband, who looked through the back bedroom window. The couple thought at first that the noise had been caused by a horse or a cow, but they could not see anything in the dark.

The Royal Oak's landlady, Eleanor Carter, deposed that the prisoners were regulars. A few days before PC Cock's murder, John and William Habron came into the public house and each had a glass of beer. As William raised his glass to take a drink, he cursed the 'bobbies', and said that if that 'bobby' (meaning Constable Cock) summoned his brother John to court for drunkenness, then he would 'do him'. On a previous occasion, she remembered John standing beside the bar window in the presence of a crowd of drinkers and saying that PC Cock had no right to summon him, as he and his brothers had done no one any harm. He added: 'If he does, by God, we will "shunt" him.' When Carter questioned him further about his 'vicious' words, he replied, 'We will shift him; he is not the first our "gaffer" (boss) has shifted and we will get him to shift him.' She told the court that the 'gaffer' was their employer Francis Deakin. Mr Cobbett commented that it must not have been the first time that she had heard an Irishman make threats over his beer. The witness made no further comment.

Market gardener Francis Deakin took the stand once again. He explained that he had built the outhouse for the brothers six years earlier and they had served him 'faithfully, honourably, and well, and had always been peaceably disposed.' He had given William the waistcoat found in the outhouse, two or three months before, into the pocket of which he recalled putting several percussion caps, after he was called out to shoot a cat, which was believed to be suffering from rabies. He said that it was likely that the caps found in the pocket by the police belonged to him and they were used in a double-barrelled shotgun. In Britain, restrictions on firearm use have been in place since the sixteenth century and, from 1870, a licence to possess a gun outside one's home was required, but could be bought easily over a Post Office counter. Francis Deakin had had his firearm for about ten years but had not used it for at least 18 months. He usually kept the cartridges locked away.

Deakin also explained that the men had to apply to him for permission to leave work, and that neither William nor his brothers, to his knowledge, had left the nursery to visit the ironmonger's in Oxford Road, which was about three and a half miles away. On that day, they had all worked until 8 pm. Deakin had left early to go to market, and returned to Chorlton just before 5 pm, by which time John had come back from the hearing for drunkenness. He saw the brothers until 6 pm, after which he went home and did not see them again that evening until he accompanied Superintendent Bent to the outhouse to make the arrests.

Superintendent Bent made no reference to the fact that Francis Deakin had described William Habron as having 'an abominable temper', when the police had arrested him. However, the police officer did mention it in his memoirs: 'It is somewhat remarkable to state that the gentleman who had at first told me that William Habron was one of the most abominable tempered fellows he ever knew, began afterwards to paint him as one of the most innocent creatures that ever walked.'

During the hearing, James Bent described the brothers' arrest again, emphasising that while they were being handcuffed, 'Frank and William Habron had become nervously excited, and that their limbs, particularly their arms, shook convulsively.' Despite their obvious fear, they did not ask the police officer why he was arresting them.

William Cobbett, acting for the defence, asked the superintendent for more details about the boot prints. He explained that the person who had made them 'had evidently been walking towards Seymour-grove.' He added that the boots of anyone walking that way on that particular evening would not have been wet and covered in mud, as it was a dry night and there was no rain after 10 pm until the following morning. However, if the person was walking along Firs Lane, towards Firs Farm, they would be 'very likely to get wet and dirty', as it was a field road with tall grass.

The case was adjourned until the following Tuesday morning.

Chapter 6

DISGRACEFUL LANGUAGE

'There is everything to show, at all events,
that William and John Habron had the strongest
feelings against the poor policeman who is dead.'

(Manchester Courier, 18 August 1876)

During the mid-nineteenth century, Irish immigration into English cities and towns peaked, in the wake of the Great Famine. Thousands of starving workers from all over Ireland, like the Habron brothers, crossed the Irish Sea, in search of shelter, food and employment. Initially, most settled in London, Liverpool and Manchester, where they formed substantial communities, occupying squalid housing in the cities' most derelict quarters, with the barest of amenities.

Between 1841 and 1851, Manchester's population rose by some 73,000, with a third of the new citizens being migrants from Ireland. By the 1850s, 15 per cent of the city's residents were of Irish origin, and a decade later they made up a fifth of the inhabitants. Despite their hopes for a better life, the migrants suffered high unemployment and dire poverty, making the Irish the largest and poorest ethnic minority at that time. Many were forced to live in the notorious cellar dwellings on the banks of the River Medlock, which became known as 'Little Ireland'. Some 20,000 people barely survived in these cramped, humid and almost subterranean rooms, with several families packed together in the worst conditions. In 1831 Dr James Kay was commissioned to investigate the dwellings: 'their narrow abodes are...always damp, and on the slightest rise of the river, which is a frequent occurrence, are flooded to the depth of several inches.' These unsanitary back-to-back cottages were filthy, set in muddy streets awash with human and animal waste. In one street, 250 residents shared an outdoor privy. Frederick Engels described their plight in his book, *The Condition of the Working Class in England*: 'in one cellar the water constantly wells up through a hole stopped with clay, the cellar lying below the river level, so that its occupant, a hand-loom weaver, had to bale out the water from his dwelling every morning and pour it into the street!'

Not surprisingly disease was rife, with killer epidemics such as cholera and typhoid sweeping through these overcrowded and unhygienic tenements. Although the back-to-back houses of Little Ireland were cleared for the construction of Oxford Road railway station in the late 1840s, the Irish remained impoverished for the rest of the century.

In the 1850s, the knowledge that one third of those receiving poor relief in the city were Irish migrants, fuelled the undercurrent of hostility and prejudice against the community. The arrival of so many unskilled workers into the city had increased the level of competition for employment and cheap housing, and lowered wages, among workers. People from all classes not only saw the Irish as a threat to Manchester's indigenous poor, but also viewed them as a health risk, referring to them with inflammatory language, such as 'vermin' and 'plague-ridden'. Furthermore, the Irish immigrants were mostly of the Catholic faith, another bone of contention during a period when many Victorians held strong prejudices against the Roman Church.

These deep-seated anti-Irish sentiments pervaded the local authorities, including the magistrates and the police. Between 1841 and 1871, 25 per cent of convicted criminals in Manchester were Irish, and in the later decades, an estimated one third of prisoners in Strangeways were Catholic. In 1872, at the height of the teenage street fighting fad known as 'scuttling', the stipendiary magistrate Charles Rickard claimed that most of the violent assaults on the streets were caused by the Irish, who were 'belligerent' and 'undisciplined'. Comments such as these perpetuated the stereotype of the Irish as lawless, too fond of drink and quick to use their fists. When the Habron brothers came from County Roscommon, Ireland to Manchester in the late 1860s, anti-Irish hatred was fiercer than ever, following the fatal shooting of Sergeant Charles Brett by members of the Irish Republican Brotherhood, also known as the Fenians.

On 11 September 1867, a vigilant police constable spotted two suspicious-looking men hanging around Smithfield Market in Manchester. The officer suspected them of planning to burgle a shop. When one of the suspects pulled a gun, they were arrested after a brief struggle. The men, who gave false names, were charged with loitering. During their detention, communication between the police in Manchester and the Irish authorities revealed their true identities: the two men were Colonel Thomas Kelly and Captain Timothy Deasy of the Irish Republican Brotherhood, and they were wanted on suspicion of terrorism. Both veterans of the American Civil War, they had come to England to take part in actions against the British government to force the issue of home rule.

On 18 September, the prisoners were to be transferred to Belle Vue Gaol, in Gorton on the edge of the city. Travelling in a horse-drawn Black Maria with other offenders, including women indicted for lesser crimes such as pickpocketing, prostitution and drunkenness, Kelly and Deasy were accompanied by Sergeant Brett, who was locked inside the van with them. Several more officers followed behind. As the convoy passed under the bridge on Hyde Road in Ardwick Green, a volley of stones hit the van forcing it to stop. The police were then quickly surrounded by armed men, who shot both the horses and wounded at least two officers. Unable to enter the locked Black Maria, the assailants screamed through the ventilation slot for the keys, which were held by Sergeant Brett. In a desperate attempt to protect the prisoners on board, especially the women, the young police officer refused to hand over the keys. A gunman poked his rifle through the slot and shot Sergeant Brett through the head. The bullet passed through his skull and lodged in his helmet.

Once they were released, Colonel Kelly and Captain Deasy fled the scene. One suspect, William O'Meara Allen, was captured soon after and within three days of the incident, the police had arrested some 50 Irish men, 26 of whom were charged. Twelve men were convicted, seven for rioting and assault, and five for the murder of Sergeant Brett. One of Brett's colleagues identified Allen as the gunman who had killed the officer.

The trial was one of the most sensational and emotive of the century and although two men were reprieved and one pardoned due to a case of mistaken identity, William Allen, Michael Larkin and Michael O'Brien were sentenced to death. On 25 November 1867, the three men were hanged and became known as the 'Manchester Martyrs'. Home Secretary Gathorne-Hardy commented that: 'What has happened will awaken Englishmen to some notion of the incendiaries around them.' After the murder of Sergeant Charles Brett, 'Fenian fever' spread like wildfire throughout Britain, causing the Victorians to fear the very real threat of Irish nationalists and their deadly campaign. When the Habron brothers faced trial for the murder of another police officer in the same city just a decade later, it was clear that the paranoia surrounding Irish violence had not abated.

The trial of John, Frank and William Habron resumed on Tuesday 15 August and was held over two days. Many of the previous witnesses repeated their evidence, and some new ones appeared in court for the first time. The bootmaker, John Leverett, who had been a juror in the coroner's court and had commented on Superintendent Bent's evidence regarding the imprint of William Habron's boot, now gave a formal testimony. While the superior police officer had been giving evidence, Leverett said he had noticed 'a peculiarity in the nailing of the boot then produced'. Using his expertise in bootmaking, he explained that the third row on the left boot was an eighth to three-eighths of an inch wider apart than the second row. This differed from the width between the corresponding rows on the right boot. He added that this was 'a very uncommon thing', and that 'it has not been a workman that has made the boots.'

The expert gunsmith William Griffiths commented on the ballistic evidence, beginning with the bullet that killed PC Cock. He reminded the jury that it was .442 size, and intended for a copper cartridge breech-loader. There was a mark on the bullet where the copper had nipped it. However, the murder weapon had still not been found. In relation to the percussion caps found in William Habron's waistcoat pocket, the gunsmith said that they were 'of the best quality', and very similar to some caps kept by Francis Deakin in a white tin box found at the property. The three caps found in the waistcoat were plain and larger than the others. This type could be purchased at an ironmonger's or a chemist's.

Francis Deakin, also referred to the percussion caps, stating that he wished to make a correction to his previous statement. He told the court that he did not keep bullets, but that it was probable that there were caps in the waistcoat when he gave it to William. Confusingly, Deakin swore that he had given a grey waistcoat to one of the brothers, but he could not remember giving them the black one found by the police.

When Deakin explained that before he had built the outhouse, the brothers used to sleep in the hayloft, one of the magistrates commented, 'I should think the pigs have a more comfortable place to sleep than that', causing laughter to erupt in the gallery. Deakin repeated his evidence about the day before PC Cock's murder, when William Habron had allegedly entered the ironmonger's to enquire about bullets. He said that it was possible his employee had left the nursery between 3 pm and 6 pm without his knowledge. After he sent William on an errand with a message for another workman around 3 pm he did not see him again until after 6pm.

The next witnesses supplied more information about the night of the murder and the brothers' alleged drinking habits. Sarah Beck Fox said that she saw John and Frank on the Thursday before the shooting and she had heard a friend, Elizabeth Whitelegge, ask John how he had fared in court on the charge of drunkenness. He had replied that his case had been deferred to the following Tuesday, adding, 'If he does me, I will do him before next Wednesday.' John had not referred to anyone by name, but Sarah Fox had believed he was talking about Constable Cock.

Elizabeth Whitelegge confirmed her friend's statement, adding that John had asked after her 'young man'. Once again, he did not mention a name, but she had assumed he was talking about PC Cock, with whom she had been 'keeping company'. This was the first time it had been revealed in court that the police officer had been involved in a relationship, but no further details were given. Wheelwright James Brownhill also saw John Habron that evening, looking 'dressed up'. When Brownhill asked him why, Habron had replied that he had been in court during the day, as his brother had been summoned by 'the little bobby'. He said that as there had been a mistake he would have to attend court again: 'If it costs me anything, I'll shoot the bastard.'

Several police officers described the night when PC Cock was murdered. Inspector John Henderson explained how he had searched the outhouse with his colleagues and found a conical-shaped bullet on the chimney mantelpiece, which was about twice the size of the one that had killed PC Cock. Henderson had also searched a box of clothing and found another percussion cap in a black waistcoat. He saw his colleague, Constable Hodgson, remove three caps from another vest pocket.

PC Charles Hodgson then described how, before entering the outhouse to arrest the Habrons, he had climbed a heap of stones by the hedge at the side of the road. From his vantage point, Hodgson had spotted a light from a candle in the Habrons' window. However, when the officers had entered the premises, they found that the light had been extinguished. The soft wax of the candle contradicted the brothers' assertion that they had been asleep in bed all evening.

PC William Ewan continued his evidence from the previous hearing, adding some fresh information. As PC Cock was being carried in the night soil cart to Dr Dill's surgery, Ewan reported hearing him say, 'They have done me this time.' Later, in the presence of more police officers, Cock had said, 'Leave me alone, Frank, you are killing me.' No one there was named 'Frank'. PC Ewan admitted that he had not disclosed this information at the coroner's inquest: 'I did not tell him all I have told you.'

When asked why, he said, 'Because I was not asked' and 'I did not think it would be of any use.' The counsel for the defence, William Cobbett, stated that this additional information could not be used in evidence against the brothers, as it had not been mentioned before. The prosecution objected but was overruled.

Sergeant Moses Thompson had been among the officers present in Dr Dill's surgery. He reported asking PC Cock three times who had shot him, to which the dying man replied, 'Let me alone and I will tell you.' Shortly afterwards, although he was 'suffering considerably', Thompson believed PC Cock had referred to a 'Frank', when he tried to speak. The final witness was Chief Constable Bruce who, as he had served in the army, was familiar with the marks of gunfire. He visited West Point the day after PC Cock's death and saw the bullet hole in the garden wall. He ordered the brick to be removed as evidence.

At the end of the hearing, the defence counsel William Cobbett conceded that 'there was some evidence to create suspicion.' However, he believed that 'there was not even a case of suspicion' against Frank Habron, despite PC Cock's apparent mention of his name. The presiding magistrate agreed and discharged Frank, who was removed from the dock. The remaining brothers, John and William, pleaded not guilty to the charge of murder, to which the magistrate replied, 'In this case an apparently cruel and cowardly assassination has been committed, and the evidence laid before us leaves us no alternative than to send you to the next assizes for trial for murder.'

The adjourned inquest into the death of PC Nicholas Cock was held on Wednesday 16 August, the same day as the final session at the police court. Once again, coroner Frederick Price presided over the meeting at the Northumberland Arms public house. John and William Habron continued to be represented by William Cobbett. Prosecuting counsel Thomas Crofton also attended, 'to watch the case on behalf of the police.' Both the deputy chief constable and Superintendent Bent were present. Many witnesses repeated their testimonies from the earlier hearings and some additional information was heard.

Ironmonger's assistant Donald McLennan, who worked in

the shop on Oxford Road where William Habron had allegedly enquired about cartridges, appeared first. He was still unable to remember whether the date had been Monday 31 July or Tuesday 1 August. McLennan repeated his assertion that his customer was the man in the dock, and added that he believed the customer to have been Irish. Furthermore, the suspect had been wearing similar clothes to the accused now in court: 'He wore a coloured shirt on both occasions, and I think I could have picked him out of a thousand men. He appeared quite collected when in the shop, and did not show any signs of excitement.' McLennan's colleague agreed with the description of the man's clothing, but was less sure about his physical appearance: 'When I saw him at the police station his hair appeared to be a little darker.' He observed, 'I thought it strange that a person should have a revolver and not know what size of cartridges he required.' Gunsmith William Griffiths shared his conclusion that the large conical-shaped bullet found by Inspector Henderson at the outhouse was from a cartridge used in a Snider Enfield rifle.

Farm labourer John Walsh added more details to his earlier statement. Walsh worked for local market gardener, John Gresty, where he was a colleague of the eldest Habron brother Thomas. He had known the Habrons for about six weeks at the time of the murder. Walsh explained that he worked opposite Francis Deakin's nursery and he saw the brothers in the garden on Tuesday 1 August. That evening, William had come to Gresty's nursery to speak to Thomas and remained there about half an hour. Between 8.30 and 9 pm, Walsh went back with John and William to their outhouse. John Habron then left for the Royal Oak to buy some tobacco, and John Walsh and William Habron went to the Lloyd's Hotel, where all three had a drink with Walsh's cousin. Both the Habron brothers remained sober. Frank Habron had stayed in bed at home. During the evening, William claimed that John Habron had remarked that he intended to keep regular hours in future. There was no mention of PC Cock.

Francis Deakin repeated his evidence from the court hearing, adding that he had never given the Habrons any bullets, and nor had he authorised them to use a firearm. They had no need for percussion caps and he had not known them to fire a weapon for any purpose. Deakin had given them secondhand clothing, but was unaware whether or not percussion caps had been left in the pockets. The market gardener said that his own bedroom was about 50 yards from the Habrons' outhouse and that he had been asleep when Superintendent Bent had woken him with news of the murder. He did not keep a dog on the premises. Deakin ended his testimony by stating that the Habrons had always been 'peaceably disposed' while they worked for him.

Many of the investigating officers were present at the inquest. PC Charles Hodgson described how he found a black waistcoat in the box at the outhouse, with three caps in a pocket, as well as a second waistcoat containing one more. He held the garments up in court, and John Habron acknowledged them to be his. PC John Gillanders, who was also present at the brothers' arrest, confirmed that William's boots were 'wet and slushy'. He admitted that they could not have got into that condition on the night PC Cock was murdered, as it was dry. Furthermore, PC Gillanders said that he had seen three boggy places in Deakin's garden nursery, which were wet during that day: the grass growing on either side of Firs Lane, which led to the farm and was 130 yards from where PC Cock was killed; and the two water courses crossing the footpaths, one of which was full of black mud.

Inspector Thomas Whitlam, Superintendent Bent's son-in-law, reminded the coroner that both William and John Habron had been summoned for drunkenness on Thursday 27 July due to information given by PC Cock. William had pleaded guilty and was fined, while John's case had been postponed to 1 August. The inquest was then adjourned to the following day.

The testimonies of the second day centred on the threats made by the Habrons to PC Cock. Sarah Fox, Elizabeth Whitelegge and James Brownhill all repeated their evidence about drinking with the brothers and overhearing them speak threateningly of the police officer. Landlady Eleanor Carter reminded the jury of the menacing statements made by both William and John Habron, that they would 'make it hot for him' if they were summoned. She also said that on the following day they had returned to the pub, saying that the police had arrested the wrong brother and that it was Frank who had been drunk. When questioned further about this new assertion, Eleanor Carter said that she had not mentioned it before as no one had asked her.

At the conclusion of all the evidence the coroner summarised the key issues to the jury. He stated that the cause of death was clear: haemorrhage from the wound to the officer's right breast and right lung, caused by a bullet from a firearm. There was no evidence to suggest suicide, but that 'a deliberate, foul, and cowardly murder' had been committed. He went on to raise the matter of PC Cock referring to 'Frank', as he was dying, offering his opinion that the officer did not necessarily know that his injury was fatal and therefore was not intending to name his killer. It was also possible that the police had mistaken the word for another, such as 'friend'.

In relation to the brothers' arrest, Mr Price found it strange that the brother who had opened the outhouse door to the police, had then returned to bed without asking the reason for their visit in the middle of the night. He also expressed his surprise that they were naked, clearly unaware that many working people in the Victorian era would have only had one change of clothes: 'I do not know whether men in their position are in the habit of lying in bed in a nude state, and, as no one has given evidence on the point, it must be dismissed as a very strange circumstance.' None of the brothers questioned the police when they were told to get out of bed, and two of them were 'excited and nervous in their manner, as if they were not entirely at ease when the arrest was made.'

The coroner reminded the court that William Habron's boots were the muddiest, which was 'a very suspicious circumstance' as, if they had stopped work at about 7 pm, then his boots should have dried out by 1 am the following morning. He asserted that the rest of the evidence was circumstantial, although William's visit to the ironmonger's was significant – if it indeed were him. There was no evidence that the men used firearms and the percussion caps found in the waistcoats could have belonged to Francis Deakin. He then moved on to examine the possible motive for the killing.

It was clear that the Habrons had been out late that night drinking, even though they claimed to have been in bed by 9.30 pm. Their motivation for killing PC Cock lay with the threats they uttered against him, overheard by several witnesses: 'I can hardly refer to the motive for the crime without considerable emotion, and on my own part I must say that I never heard such disgraceful language used by men before...The disgraceful language shows they entertained a deadly hatred to the man.'

Frederick Price ended by saying that it was likely that Frank Habron had been in bed at the time of the murder, as confirmed by many of the witnesses' testimonies, and he informed the court that he had already been discharged by the police. After a brief consultation lasting 15 minutes, the jury returned a guilty verdict against John and William, and the case was referred to the Manchester Assizes. The prisoners were removed to the cells, where they would remain for the next three months, awaiting their final trial at the criminal court for murder.

Chapter 7

'A COLD-BLOODED TRAGEDY'

'It appeared...a most startling thing that at so
short a distance from Manchester, and in one of
the most respectable suburbs of the town, in a
public highway, well lighted...a policeman could
have been shot down in his duty.'

(Manchester Courier, 28 November 1876)

In 1876, the Winter Assizes in Manchester opened on Friday
24 November, overseen by Mr Justice Lindley and Mr Justice
Lopes. There were 69 prisoners on the list, which included five
cases of murder and more minor offences such as burglary,
conspiracy to defraud, assault, forgery and concealment of
birth. John and William Habron were entered on the calendar of
prisoners for the sessions as aged 23 and 18 years respectively,
their occupation recorded as 'gardener'. It was also noted that
their education was 'imperfect', although unlike many of their
contemporaries, they were literate. The brothers were to appear
before Sir Nathaniel Lindley, an experienced judge who had
received a knighthood the previous year on his appointment to
Her Majesty's High Court of Justice.

At 10.30 am, on Monday 27 November, Mr Justice Lindley
took his seat on the bench. The court was packed with spectators
and, as the public gallery was full, there was a large crowd

waiting outside. This time, the prisoners were to be defended by Mr Leresche, with Mr Higgin and Mr Addison acting for the prosecution. John Henry Proctor Leresche was an experienced barrister with over 30 years at the bar. Known for his tenacious cross-examinations and patience with recalcitrant witnesses, 'no case, however paltry, was too insignificant to engage his full attention' (*Manchester Courier*, 7 March 1894). A Freemason and regular church-goer, he was a supporter of many charities. Although legal aid was not fully provided for those with low incomes until 1903, towards the end of the nineteenth century it was granted to individuals charged with murder. Therefore, it is likely that at this stage in the Habrons' case that their defence was paid for by the state.

Mr Higgin opened by giving a summary of the alleged crime. He described how PC Nicholas Cock had been walking his beat when he was shot; the Habron brothers' subsequent arrest; and the evidence against them. The barrister noted that the deceased was 'a very active officer, punctual in the discharge of his duties and...anxious to commend himself to the consideration of his superior officers'. After presenting the evidence to the jury, Mr Higgin exhorted them to give the defendants the benefit of 'any reasonable doubt', but to remember that the victim was a public servant, and to take the matter 'into their most serious consideration', in order that the outcome of the case quieten public fears.

The case for the prosecution began with a local architect, who produced a map of the spot where PC Cock was killed. It was marked with all the buildings and roads in the vicinity of West Point, as well as the position of the gas lamps and the distances between the key locations, measured in feet. Watchmaker Frederick Wilcox was the first to testify. He described how, when he had returned John Habron's watch after cleaning it, three months before PC Cock's murder, John Habron had threatened to shoot the police officer. Mr Leresche for the defence, pointed out that, despite Mr Wilcox being a postman, as well as a watchmaker, and therefore used to delivering the post on certain days, he could not remember the date on which he had returned the watch to the defendant.

The following two witnesses also spoke of the threats

made by the brothers to the police officer. Eleanor Carter, the beerhouse keeper's wife said that the brothers were sober when they made the threats and that John 'seemed very bitter'. Wheelwright James Brownhill reported how the brothers had spoken aggressively of PC Cock on the day of their court summons, but added that he had not thought they meant any real harm. Mr Leresche suggested that 'the general impression in the neighbourhood was that the deceased was too officious.'

Next in the stand was Elizabeth Whiteley, a local laundress, who had been courting Nicholas Cock until around a month before his death. Whiteley had seen John Habron in the Royal Oak on the afternoon of PC Cock's murder. Her testimony was followed by those who had been present at the time of the shooting, including a new witness. Nathaniel Williams, a travelling salesman who had been at West Point at 11.50 pm on 1 August, told the court that he had seen a man standing by the gate at the corner of Firs Lane, but could not identify him.

Law student John Massey Simpson described once again how he and PC Cock had met at the 'jutting stone', which marked the end of the officer's beat, near to the junction. He told the jury that he saw a man 'walking out of the darkness' under a lamp at the corner of Seymour Grove and Upper Chorlton Road, who 'seemed to falter and hesitate as to which way he should go.' The stranger was dressed in a brown coat and wearing a round, low hat, but Simpson did not recognise him. When he attended the police station the following day, he saw a man sitting in the inspector's chair, also wearing a brown coat but without a hat. Later, the man crossed the room in front of him and Simpson noted that he was stooped and similar in appearance to the man he had seen in the shadows at West Point. Simpson admitted that he had thought that the man under the lamp had been elderly, because of his general appearance. Otherwise, the resemblance between him and William Habron was close. The defence observed that the coat and hat were 'of the ordinary kind'.

In contradiction to Simpson, PC James Beanland stated that he believed the man they had both seen that night was about 22 years old and 'of fresh complexion'. The suspect had walked erect, was about 5 feet 7 inches tall and was wearing dark coloured clothing. When he saw William Habron in court, PC Beanland said he believed him to be this man. When questioned further, PC Beanland admitted that he could not swear that William was the man glimpsed on the night of the murder. However, his description of PC Cock's shooting was corroborated by several more witnesses, including the night soil men and the first police officers to arrive at the scene.

After some discussion between the barristers and the judge as to whether the statement made by PC Cock while he was dying should be admissible in court, Mr Justice Lindley deferred to the defence, who asked Sergeant Moses Thompson to repeat what he had heard his injured colleague say. He attested that PC Cock had addressed him as 'Frank', although there was no person present of that name, and Mr Higgin suggested postponing Sergeant Thompson's evidence. Dr Dill gave the details of the post-mortem examination, after which the court adjourned for lunch.

Following the break, Superintendent Bent took the stand, after having been described by the prosecution as 'one of the most respectable and active officers in the force'. He recounted how, after receiving news of the shooting, he had sent his officers straight to the outhouse where the Habron brothers lived: 'I suspected the three Habrons from the first.' Following PC Cock's death, he arrested the brothers, noting that 'they did not appear to be like men who had just woken out of sleep.' He had noticed that William's boots were 'slutchy' and very wet and he had found a soft, recently extinguished candle. The senior police officer reminded the jury that although he had not mentioned a time or place of the murder to the brothers, John had said immediately that he was in bed at the time. Bent then described having proceeded to West Point, where he discovered the incriminating footprints. Superintendent Bent's testimony was supported by seven other police officers, including his son-in-law Inspector Whitlam. Sergeant Thompson added that, when the prisoners were arrested, they 'hung down their heads and trembled very much.'

The prosecution then moved on to establishing the Habron brothers' whereabouts before the shooting. Labourer John

Walsh and barmaid Ann Cavers both confirmed that William and John were drinking in the Lloyd's Hotel for about half an hour, until around 10 pm. A new witness, farm labourer Henry Ayton, said that he saw the brothers leave about 10.30 pm. Everyone agreed that Frank Habron had been in bed all evening, or at least that he had not been seen out and about. Local market gardener's wife, Mary Brundreth, and 11-year-old Edward Blakeley testified that they heard noises between 12 and 1 am.

The Habrons' employer, Francis Deakin, gave further details about the brothers' service in his market garden. William had worked for him for seven years, Frank for eight and John for nine. During the afternoon of 1 August, they were engaged in tying up lettuces and picking raspberries and he did not see them after 5.30 pm. Deakin trusted the brothers enough to regularly leave William in charge of the nursery, and send him out with messages. He repeated his view that they were 'very peaceable men'.

The final witnesses for the prosecution included ironmonger Donald McLennan, who claimed he had discussed the cost of cartridges with William Habron in his shop. He had not the least doubt as to the prisoner's identity this time and had taken him for an Irishman because of his accent. His colleague corroborated his statement. Gunsmith William Griffiths and bootmaker John Leverett both gave summaries of their evidence relating to the fatal bullet and the footprints found at the scene.

John Henry Leresche said that he had several witnesses for the defence, and that he felt 'a great responsibility resting upon him'. He asked the judge for an adjournment to the following day, which was granted.

Mr Justice Lindley opened the second day of the trial at 10 am. Mr Leresche announced that he had taken advantage of the break to re-assess the defence's position and planned to call witnesses who could testify about the events of Tuesday 1 August, now that the ironmonger's colleague had verified that the man thought to be William Habron had called into the shop on that day, rather than Monday 31 July.

Gardener William Kelsall was the first to take the stand. He also worked in Francis Deakin's nursery and had known the defendants for three months. On Tuesday 1 August, Kelsall went to Shudehill Market, about four miles away, returning around 2.20 pm, accompanied by Frank and John Habron, who had been on their way back from court. They stopped for a glass of ale at a public house. When all three men entered Deakin's yard at 4 pm, they encountered William Habron. Kelsall saw William later, first in the stables and then in the field pulling lettuces, where he worked until about 6 pm. William Kelsall left work at this time and did not see the brothers again that evening. He concluded his statement by saying, 'The prisoners had always borne the character of being quiet, peaceable men.' They had never threatened him, nor had he heard them threaten PC Cock. Kelsall had always been on good terms with them.

Another of Deakin's employees, James Crossgrove, said that he was working in the gardens that day, from 6 am until late at night. He recalled that Frank and John Habron had left for the police court at 10 am, after which he had continued working in the fields with William Habron. They gathered raspberries and tied lettuces until 5 pm. The Habrons remained at the nursery until 8 pm. Mr Higgin, the prosecuting barrister, asked Crossgrove about the statement he had given earlier to the police, specifically whether Inspector Henderson had written down what he said. Crossgrove replied that he had. Higgin asked him if he could read and write, and the witness admitted that he could not, and that he had signed his statement with his mark, a cross. Mr Higgin then read out the statement in court, in which James Crossgrove had said that he had been tying lettuces with the Habrons on either Monday or Tuesday, but he could not remember which day. Crossgrove replied that it had been 'put down wrong'.

The next witness for the defence was Winifred Foyd, who also worked for Francis Deakin. She was at the nursery all day on Tuesday 1 August and saw William Habron there in the morning. She remembered Frank and John returning with William Kelsall during the afternoon. When Foyd left at 6 pm, William was still there. As with the previous witness, her original statement to the police had noted her uncertainty as to whether it had been Monday or Tuesday. Winifred Foyd was also illiterate and had signed the police book with a cross.

Two more of Deakin's employees testified. Catherine Conlan, a labourer's wife, was present on Tuesday 1 August and had seen William Habron tying lettuces all day. Mary O'Brien was working with the other women that day and confirmed their statements. According to all the testimonies from William Habron's colleagues, he had not left the nursery on Tuesday 1 August and therefore could not have been the customer asking about cartridges in the ironmonger's shop. The defence ended with two character witnesses. Dr Rains, a local GP, said that he had known the Habrons for five or six years, and considered them to be, 'very peaceable, well-conducted men'. Market gardener John Gresty, for whom Thomas Habron worked, said the same.

John Henry Leresche then addressed the jury, picking up on the points raised by his colleague, Mr Higgin, about fears for public safety in the neighbourhood: 'it was an awful thing to contemplate that, at so short a distance from the very centre of Manchester, an outrage of this character should have been committed.' He added that it was also 'an awful thing' to be on trial for one's life, and urged the jury to consider whether the evidence given by the prosecution was conclusive enough for such a serious case of murder and to proceed only 'on the surest and the most stable ground'. Leresche suggested that the alleged motive of the previous convictions was not sufficient, as PC Cock had not testified in the hearing for drunkenness against the two Habron brothers, and that William had pleaded guilty at once. In relation to the threats uttered against the police officer, he opined that they were due to 'a rash, and a random, and a coarse way of speaking', but that there was no real malice intended. Furthermore, only once was William overheard making any threats. The cumulative testimony from multiple witnesses might have made it seem to the jury as though it had happened more frequently. The barrister concluded that: 'All the threats were frivolous, and not the indications of a lurking revenge against the deceased.'

Next Mr Leresche addressed the question as to the identity of the suspicious man seen at the time of the murder, noting that the evidence was based on a 'resemblance' between him and William Habron. He outlined the differences in the description of the man given by John Massey Simpson and PC James Beanland, concluding that, 'the evidence of these witnesses was evidence which, when fairly weighed, failed to maintain the identity of the prisoner.' He then commented on the chain of evidence, including the light in the outhouse, which he said could have been extinguished for many reasons. He reminded the jury that the condition of William's boots could be accounted for by the state of the garden in which the brothers worked. Leresche noted that the seemingly incriminating comment made by John Habron at the time of his arrest was explained by 'the position the men were placed in by a midnight visit from a posse of police, and probably partially due to the fact that, being an Irishman he was voluble, according to the habit of his countrymen.'

As for the footprint, he pointed out to the jury that 'it would not be safe to convict a man of the terrible crime of murder upon evidence so unsatisfactory as that with regard to the footprint.' He concluded by saying that the strongest circumstance in favour of the defendants was that no murder weapon had been found in their possession. The court adjourned for lunch.

When the trial resumed, Mr Higgin opened his summary for the prosecution by asserting: 'That a cruel murder had been committed, no one could doubt at all'. If the defendants were proved not to be the culprits, he argued, then they must persist in their investigations until the real killer was caught whilst, 'enduring the fear that a peaceable person walking down the Chorlton-road in the night time was in danger of being shot.' Acknowledging the circumstantial nature of the evidence, he exhorted the jury to consider the whole picture, in order to make a reasonable judgment, including the threats and the footprints. In reference to the witness statements given for the defence, Mr Higgin said that 'the prisoners were Irishmen, and, although he did not mean to say that it was not possible for an Irishman to tell the truth, at the same time it was natural to suppose that the witnesses, two or three of whom were Irish, would sympathise with their fellow countrymen in the dock.' Higgin felt that there was no excuse for William Habron's inflammatory language which, he added without any evidence, was commonplace in Ireland.

Mr Justice Lindley emphasised the importance of the case, especially as a police officer had been murdered 'without any immediate provocation', such as a riot or disturbance of any kind, implying that the killer had no 'excuse'. It was in the general public's interest that his killer should be brought to justice. The jury, he stressed, had to consider whether the case was one in which there was 'reasonable' certainty of both or one of the prisoners' guilt. The judge reminded them that it was not unreasonable that suspicion had fallen on the brothers following the threats they had issued towards the police officer. Yet, he urged them to take all the evidence into account: 'it was by the multitude of evidence or facts all warranting the same inference, all pointing in the same direction, that rendered circumstantial evidence trustworthy.'

At 4.55 pm, the jury retired to make their decision. They returned after two and a half hours of deliberation and delivered their verdicts to the crowded courtroom. The foreman announced that they had found John Habron 'not guilty', but they had found his brother, William, 'guilty, with a strong recommendation to mercy on account of his youth'. John Habron left the dock.

Defendants were not allowed to testify until 1898, and their only opportunity to address the court was prior to sentencing. The clerk of the arraigns turned to William for his response to the verdict, saying: 'Have you anything to say now why sentence of death should not be passed upon you according to law?' William replied in a faint voice, 'I am innocent of it.' Mr Justice Lindley put on the black cap and, saying that the matter of mercy was now in the hands of Her Majesty's government, passed the death sentence. According to the *Manchester Courier*, William 'appeared to be greatly agitated, and for a few moments seemed utterly unable to realise the terrible position in which he stood.' Very pale and slowly raising his hands, he clutched nervously at the dock rail, saying in a tremulous voice and with a strong Irish accent, 'Let me speak one word.' Two warders took hold of him, telling him that he had to leave the dock. William looked at them, at the jury, then finally at the judge, and said, 'I am innocent.' He was then removed from the court to await his punishment.

Chapter 8

WILLIAM HABRON'S LAST HOPE

'If ever an act was carefully planned, and
deliberately executed, it was this piece of revenge.'

(London Daily News, 30 November 1876)

The murder of PC Cock and the subsequent conviction of
William Habron were not widely reported at the time. Apart
from the Manchester press, most other regional and national
newspapers paid the killing scant regard, with merely a
paragraph or two outlining the facts of the case. The *London
Daily News* was one of the only publications to print the
full details of the story, pointing out to its readers that the
offence was 'unusual', and that the evidence was 'made up
out of a number of small details'. It conceded that the case
was a very perplexing one, especially for the jury, as there was
little evidence of Habron's motive for such a 'very striking and
serious' crime. However, the cumulative effect of the 'extremely
circumstantial' evidence was powerful enough to convict the
young labourer.

The newspaper concluded its report with a warning to police
officers, who ran great risks in their duty 'from the passions of
revengeful and violent men'. Constables were accustomed to
facing attacks during street riots and often received threats, but
the paper felt this crime was of a much graver nature: 'It is one

thing to help to kick a policeman to death in the confusion of a night broil, and quite another to frame deliberate plots against his life.' For this reason, the journalist opined, the police must be protected and William Habron's conviction would serve as a deterrent for those tempted to imitate him.

On Friday 1 December, the *Manchester Courier* published its final summary, after reporting on the case since the summer. It concluded that 'there was cunning and deliberation which invested the tragedy with some degree of mystery.' Praise followed for the police who had 'nothing to show who had perpetrated the deed', especially for Superintendent James Bent who had unravelled the case 'with remarkable skill and success'. The newspaper had little sympathy for Habron, now facing a death sentence, as 'the cold-blooded tragedy' was 'deliberately and craftily carried out'. William Habron may only have been 18 years old, but he 'was not too young to harbour feelings of deadly revenge, to track his victim cautiously in the night, and to deliberately take his life.' Repealing his sentence would send the wrong message to other would-be killers.

The same paper carried a letter to the editor from one of the jurors. Without giving his name, he (women could not serve on a jury until 1921) outlined the reasons for the jury's decision: 'the jury were immensely influenced by the footprint...it came out strongly that this footprint was exactly like William's boot.' He also revealed that ten out of the twelve jurors had initially voted to return a guilty verdict, which led to the recommendation for mercy. This was followed by another letter on the subject from William Henry Gaskell, a hat shop owner from Hulme. He felt that the two and a half hours taken by the jury to make their decision was insufficient, due to the case being complicated with contradictory evidence, and he also raised the question of the missing murder weapon. He ended his communication with a plea for steps to be taken in consideration of 'the unfortunate and condemned youth'. Many others shared his concerns and a campaign to save William Habron from the gallows was already underway.

The following Monday, the *Manchester Courier* reported that the date of Habron's execution was likely to be set for a fortnight's time, despite the fact that a petition to the home secretary had already been initiated by his original defence solicitor, William Cobbett. Throughout the next week, advertisements appeared in the local press urging people to sign the petition for Habron's reprieve, which was available in the offices of Cobbett, Wheeler and Cobbett, in central Manchester. More letters had been published along the lines that the verdict was not justified by the evidence. One impassioned letter-writer was local stationer Albert Megson, who was desperate to save the young man's life: 'The dreadful thought of an innocent man being put to death, and the mysteries which seem to shroud this particular case, induces me to ask assistance...with a view at all events of obtaining a reprieve.'

Those sympathetic to Habron's cause met on Wednesday 6 December at the Clarence Hotel, Manchester, to discuss his plight. Some 40 gentlemen attended the meeting and Mr R. Seed took the chair. Albert Megson tabled the first resolution to present a memorial (a statement of facts) to the home secretary requesting a reconsideration of the sentence. Megson pointed out to the group that this was not a question about the justification of the death penalty, but a case in which there was no evidence to support such a harsh punishment. The resolution was accepted and a sub-committee undertook to draft the petition. The paper simply asked the home secretary to review the case, because of the circumstantial nature of the evidence against William Habron: 'we trust that you will be led to the conclusion that the evidence in this case was too weak to warrant the capital sentence.' The meeting further agreed that the public should be invited to sign the petition and that copies would be placed in businesses and shops throughout the city. Mr Megson was appointed treasurer and began requesting subscriptions to cover their costs.

By this time, the first petition held at the solicitors' office had been signed by some 2,000 people, including the mayor of Manchester Alderman Heywood, and Jacob Bright, the newly-returned MP for South West Manchester. Addressed to Home Secretary Richard Assheton Cross, the memorial opened with a declaration of the facts of the case, followed by a request for review due to 'insufficient and inadequate evidence...based on one single footprint.' It also drew attention to the fact that most of the witnesses for the prosecution were the victim's fellow police officers. A spokesperson for the Home Office responded that the memorial would receive Mr Cross's 'careful consideration'.

Whilst the heated discussion about Habron's conviction was taking place in the newspapers, Mr Justice Lindley, who had meted out the fatal sentence, sent for Chief Constable Bruce of the Lancashire Constabulary, Superintendent Bent and PC Beanland. The judge expressed his 'great satisfaction' at the way in which the police had handled the case, which he had reported to the home secretary. Following the meeting, the constabulary's chief clerk wrote to the Home Office, recalling the meeting and pointing out 'how highly such an expression of opinion from such a source should be valued.'

Following his conviction, William Habron was held in the condemned cell at Strangeways, where he was attended by the prison chaplain, receiving the priest's ministrations 'in a reverent spirit'. He attended Mass on Sunday in the Roman Catholic chapel and 'manifested a fully devotional spirit'. Habron consistently protested his innocence of the 'dastardly crime', yet remained 'very sanguine' about his position and was confident of obtaining a reprieve.

Throughout the following week, more letters were sent to the Home Office, but the only communications received by return were formal acknowledgements of receipt. On Friday 15 December, William's aunt, Mrs Cosgrove and four of his brothers, including John and Frank, visited him in prison. The local press reported that 'the interview was of a very affecting character', especially as it was assumed that the execution would take place after the weekend. Shortly after, John left England to return home to Ireland. The *Manchester Courier* also revealed that Habron's friends back home had not been over to visit him 'being too much distressed by the position in which he is placed' – it is more likely that they could not afford the journey, after assisting the brothers with the defence. The condemned man continued to receive the chaplain's attentions and expressed 'great hope of being reprieved'.

On Monday 18 December, it was announced that William

Habron's execution would take place in three days' time. This prompted Hugh Birley, one of the three MPs for Manchester to write to the home secretary. He received the same curt response as the others. However, on Tuesday, just two days before William Habron was due to be hanged, the home secretary finally granted him the reprieve that everyone had been waiting for. At 5 pm, the Home Office sent a telegraph to Captain Leggett, governor of Strangeways Prison, who immediately communicated the news to the prisoner. At first, William Habron 'did not seem to realise his altered position', as although he had been protesting his innocence, he had become 'perfectly resigned to his fate'. Once the news had sunk in, he 'manifested much joy at his life being spared', and wrote to his parents in Ireland.

Despite the jubilation of Habron's supporters, other members of the public were not so happy about his respite, fearing that it might encourage others to contemplate murder, and more letters arrived at the Home Office protesting at the decision. One resident of Whalley Range, where the murder took place, wrote of his fear that the reprieve would 'work a frightful mischief' as, according to him, the 'Papist Party' had publicly vowed to 'take away the life of officers on watch'. He ended his letter by exhorting the home secretary to be firm in his action against 'the curse of these deluded Papists'.

Two weeks later, on 30 December, a public memorial to PC Nicholas Cock was unveiled in the graveyard of the parish church in Chorlton-cum-Hardy where the officer was buried. The 'very handsome' headstone cost £60 (worth about £5,000 today), which was raised by public subscription. Made of Aberdeen granite, the headstone was of a classical design with a double base. The upper base bore the insignia of the deceased officer's rank, with his helmet, belt, gloves, lamp and staff, all carved in white marble. On the pediment were the arms and crest of the county of Lancashire. The inscription read: 'To the memory of Nicholas Cock, an able and energetic officer of the county constabulary, who, on 2 August 1876, while engaged in the faithful discharge of his duty, was cruelly assassinated'.

Some 60 members of the Manchester Division attended

the ceremony, including Superintendent Bent. The Reverend Canon Crace gave an address, lamenting that PC Cock was 'barely 21 years' and that he had only been in the force for a few months, when he was 'foully murdered'. He said that although Constable Cock's life had been short, it had been 'fruitful'. The officer's devotion to his duty would bring solace to his family, he hoped, and would encourage his colleagues to give greater loyalty to the general public, who 'so completely depended on them for their protection and for their safety.' Canon Crace ended by blessing the police force and asking if he could contribute to the cost of the memorial.

Meanwhile, William Habron had been spared the gallows, but his fate was still uncertain. Now known only as Prisoner C 1547, he remained alone in the condemned cell, waiting further instruction from the home secretary. The *Manchester Courier* reported: 'no change has been manifested in Habron's demeanour, and he still clings to the hope he will be reprieved, but not with so much confidence as he first exhibited.' On 8 January 1877, his brother John wrote from Ireland to one of William's supporters, Joseph Lomas, a resident of Pendleton, Salford. John, who was now staying with his parents in Cloonfad, County Roscommon, declared in his letter that neither he nor his brother William 'never had anything to do with that dastardly crime'. He thanked Mr Lomas and the other gentlemen for supporting William, and asked if there was anything else they could do 'to get him out of his misery'. The family had no money left, as they had spent everything they had on the brothers' defence. Mr Lomas informed the newspapers and passed the letter on to the home secretary.

John Habron's plea went unanswered. Since his brother's trial at the end of November, while he was still living in Manchester, John had been overheard using violent language aimed at three chief witnesses in the case. In the light of his alleged threats, the magistrates and chief constable had issued an order authorising the arming of police on night duty in the township of Chorlton-cum-Hardy, with cutlasses. They had also increased the number of officers patrolling the neighbourhood from two to six, with the men now walking their beat in pairs.

This may be the reason why John left England so quickly after his brother's death sentence was reprieved.

On 3 February 1877, the *Manchester Times* announced that the home secretary had informed the governor of Strangeways Prison that William Habron's death sentence had been commuted to penal servitude for life. According to the newspaper, William 'appeared much disappointed' at the news. He was finally removed from the condemned cell to wait for a transfer to another institution.

On hearing the news, John Habron wrote to Joseph Lomas again, protesting his brother's innocence and thanking his loyal supporters. He described how his family had been left 'in trouble and misery' after spending all their money on 'a poor case'. John ended the letter with the hope that the true perpetrator would be found and that 'Providence soon will show their guilt'.

On 15 February, William was transferred to Pentonville Prison in London, and from there moved to Millbank Prison two days later. Millbank opened in 1821 and, for much of its history, was used as a holding facility for convicts waiting to be transported to penal colonies overseas. By 1877, transportation had ended. Arrivals to Millbank Prison underwent a short period of solitary confinement and, after nine months to one year of imprisonment, male convicts were usually transferred to a public works prison, where prisoners provided labour for local projects, such as excavating quarries. William Habron was eventually sent to Portland, located on an island off the coast of Dorset.

Whilst still in Millbank, William Habron sent his own petition to the home secretary. With poor grammar and full of errors, the letter was addressed directly to Queen Victoria, as she had spared his life. Habron requested the queen to offer a reward, in order to find the real killer. To that end, he gave her his own account of what had happened on 2 August 1876, when PC Cock was shot. As he had not been allowed to testify in court, this was the first time he had the chance to give his version of events. The details in the letter were confusing and badly expressed. William began by claiming that a night watchman had shot the police officer. He named the culprit as

'John Hennery Simson', close to the name of the law student who found the wounded police officer. He then suggested that 'Simson' had placed the blame on him, along with 'PC Beenland'. He conceded that if 'Simson' was not guilty, then he must have bribed someone else to shoot PC Cock, as 'ther is plenty in that neighbourhood that would take a mans life for very little [*sic*].'

William Habron then gave his opinion of the witnesses in the case, arguing that they had threatened him and his brothers, rather than the other way around. The list included Wilcox the watchmaker and Brownhill the wheelwright, who had both testified against them. According to William, the aggravation between James Brownhill and John Habron was caused by the former having committed adultery with the wife of one of Francis Deakin's servants. This incident had led to the summons for drunkenness at the end of July. William also claimed that Superintendent Bent had made the bootprints himself to implicate him. At the end of his rambling account, William Habron asked the queen to put up a reward of £100 to find the real murderer: 'it will deliver me out of prison and it will rease me out of poverty the remender of my life [*sic*].'

However, as far as the authorities were concerned, the case was closed. Superintendent Bent had been awarded the largest sum permissible of £3, (worth about £250 today) 'for the energy and untiring zeal he displayed in bringing to justice William Habron.' Colonel Bruce had resigned as chief constable of Lancashire Constabulary, after being offered the position of deputy inspector-general of police in Ireland. William Habron was left to serve out his life sentence in prison, and nothing more was heard for two years, until another condemned man made a startling confession.

Chapter 9

SAVED FROM THE SHADOWS

"'A complex mind," said Holmes. "All great
criminals have that. My old friend Charlie Peace
was a violin virtuoso.'"

*(The Adventure of the Illustrious Client, Sir Arthur Conan
Doyle, 1924)*

Whilst William Habron was languishing in prison, the Home
Office received a number of confessions from individuals
claiming to have murdered PC Cock. In early 1877, Henry E.
Martell wrote twice to the editor of the *Manchester Evening
News,* from America: 'I confess iam the man who shot And
Murdered Police Nicholas Cock...Ihope iwill be forgiven Iwish to
Make Aware of it [*sic*]'. The newspaper passed the information
to the authorities, who were required to investigate each new
assertion. However, two more years later, one unexpected
confession finally posed a serious challenge to William's
conviction.

On 17 February 1879, convicted murderer Charlie Peace
penned a statement to the home secretary. Peace was awaiting
execution at Armley Gaol, Leeds for murdering his former
lover's husband. Peace wrote that he had been present at the
Habrons' trial in Manchester, on 27 November 1876, and that
he knew William Habron to be innocent, because he had shot

Constable Cock, not Habron.

Charles Frederick Peace was born in Sheffield on 15 May 1832, the fourth child of John and Jane Peace. Originally a miner, John Peace had lost one of his legs in a colliery accident, after which he joined Wombwell's Travelling Menagerie as a trainer, being a keen animal lover. John eventually returned to Sheffield, where he was working as a shoemaker at the time of Charles's birth in 1832. All the Peace children received a basic education and young Charles, known as Charlie, inherited a love of music from his father, becoming a talented violinist. Known locally as the 'modern Paganini', Charlie performed in music halls and public houses. He also learnt magic tricks to entertain his audiences.

From the age of 14, Charlie worked in a steelworks as a roller. During his first year of employment, he too suffered a serious accident, when a bolt of molten steel pierced his leg below the knee. Charlie's leg was saved although he was left with a pronounced limp. Towards the end of the 1840s, John Peace died and in 1851 the census shows that Charlie was living with his mother in the home of John Greer, a glass and china dealer, in Kingston-upon-Hull.

Charlie Peace was convicted for the first time in 1851. Aged 19, he served a one-month prison sentence for burglary, after the police found stolen goods at his home. Three years later, more stolen items were discovered in the family home and Peace was tried in Doncaster for larceny on 10 October 1854. Due to his previous conviction, as well as an earlier charge of vagrancy, he received a four-year sentence. On his release, Peace began travelling further afield to break into houses, committing many offences in other towns in the north-west. Often changing his appearance, he would climb onto a porch or shin up a drainpipe, entering the property through an upstairs window. He allegedly carried the tools he used for burglary in his violin case.

During the next two decades, by day Charlie Peace ran a legitimate business as a picture framer, while by night he returned to housebreaking to supplement his income. He also adopted the practice of carrying a loaded firearm, and accidentally shot off two of his own fingers when reaching into his pocket. Despite using several aliases, Peace served further long stretches in prison for theft, including six years in Strangeways, and eight in Wakefield Prison, from which he tried unsuccessfully to escape. After his aborted bid for freedom, he was transferred to Millbank, then to Chatham and even sent to Gibraltar, as were many male convicts at the time. When he was finally released in the early 1870s, he returned to Sheffield to join his wife and daughter.

In between prison sentences, in 1865 Peace married Hannah Ward (née Hanes), a young widow with a son known as 'Willie'. The couple had two children: Jane born in 1863 and John Charles two years later. During the final year of Charlie's incarceration in Wakefield Prison, on 25 November 1865 six-year-old John Charles died of smallpox. He was buried in Burngreave Cemetery, Sheffield.

In 1874, Charlie moved his family to a new house in Darnall, a suburb in eastern Sheffield mostly populated by steelworkers. The Peace family attended the local church, where the vicar was Reverend J. H. Littlewood, former chaplain of Wakefield Prison during Peace's imprisonment there. Two doors down from the Peace family in Britannia Road, lived Katherine and Arthur Dyson. Katherine, known as 'Kate', was originally from Ireland but moved to America with her parents, where she later met Arthur, while he was working on the railways there. The couple returned to England, settling in Sheffield about the same time as the Peace family arrived in Darnall. They had one infant son. The two couples struck up a friendship and regularly socialised together.

After a while, Arthur Dyson began to notice a closeness developing between his wife and Charlie, so he tried to distance the pair by reducing visits and dissuading Peace from spending time with Katherine. Despite his efforts, Charlie and Katherine embarked on an affair. When Arthur lost his job and was at home more often, he discovered that notes were being passed between the lovers. Arthur sent a note to Charlie asking him to keep away from his wife, but it didn't stop them. By 1876, the affair had begun to cool, but the relationship between the two men had become increasingly hostile. On one occasion, after a quarrel, Charlie held a revolver to Arthur's head and threatened to shoot him. Although Dyson applied for a restraining order against Peace, he decided to move his family to another part of the city.

On the 29 November, the day after the Habrons' trial in Manchester, with his emotions heightened after being present in court, Charlie returned to Sheffield and went in pursuit of Katherine. Late at night, he waited outside the couple's new house in Banner Cross, standing on their back wall, until she stepped out into the yard to go to the privy. As soon as Katherine saw Charlie in the shadows, she began to threaten him. Peace pulled out his revolver and held it to her face saying, 'Now, you be careful what you are saying to me; you know me of old, and know what I can do. I am not a man to be talked to in that way.' Katherine screamed and her husband came running out of the house into the yard. Peace tried to run down the passage leading back to the main road, but Dyson seized him. There was a struggle and Peace shouted, 'Stand back, and let me go.' He fired his revolver. The shot missed Arthur and he seized Charlie, grabbing the arm that held the gun. Peace fired again and this time Arthur received a bullet to the head. He died later of his injuries, but by then Charlie Peace had fled.

As Peace ran from the scene of the shooting, a packet of letters slipped out of his pocket. They later confirmed his identity as Arthur Dyson's killer. The police circulated his description in the *Police Gazette*: 'he is thin and slightly built, 46 years of age, but looks 10 years older, 5 feet 4 or 5 inches high, grey (nearly white) hair, beard, and whiskers.' Two fingers on his left hand were missing and he walked 'with his legs rather wide apart.' In additional to a list of Peace's known aliases, the description included details of his businesses as a picture framer and dealer, and a watch repairer, his previous convictions, the cities in which he had lived, as well as 'associates with loose women'. It ended with an appeal for any information to be sent to the chief constable of Sheffield.

After Arthur Dyson's death, Peace was forced to move around constantly to avoid arrest, whilst his family remained in Sheffield. Peace changed his appearance by applying walnut oil to his face and hands to darken his complexion, and dyeing his grey hair. He could also dislocate his jaw at will, due to a fracture some years earlier, which gave him a protruding chin. The fugitive even made a tube in which to insert his left arm with its tell-tale fingers, adding a hook to the end, so that it resembled an artificial hand. While on the run in early 1877, Peace met Susan Grey (also known as Bailey) in Nottingham. A former music hall singer, she had previous convictions for theft. Despite both being married (Susan was estranged from her husband), they became lovers and moved around together.

After a brief stay in Hull, the pair returned to Nottingham, where Peace adopted the alias John Ward, and Susan Grey was known as either Mrs Thompson or Mrs Ward. When, once again, they came to the attention of the local police, the couple moved to London. In 1878, Peace was living with Susan in Peckham, when he was joined by his wife and stepson, as well as their daughter and her husband, after which they all lived together. Peace set up in business as an antiques dealer, using the name 'Thompson'.

At 2 am on 10 October, whilst Charlie was burgling a house in Blackheath, a passing police officer on night duty noticed a light flickering in the drawing room at the back of the house. PC Edward Robinson watched as the light moved from room to room. One of his colleagues rang the doorbell to see if the occupants were at home, but there was no answer and the light was extinguished. Moments later, Peace leapt out of the drawing room window into the garden. Robinson, who had been standing on the garden wall, jumped down, breaking some glass in his fall. The noise alerted Peace who began to run towards the bottom of the garden. Robinson followed him and, as he gave chase, Peace pulled out his revolver.

The police officer stopped. He was about six yards away from Peace and, as it was a moonlit night, he could see the gun clearly. Peace said, 'Keep back, keep off, or by God I will shoot you.' Robinson replied, 'You had better not.' Peace fired three chambers of his revolver: two bullets passed to the left of PC Robinson's head and the third went over him. Undeterred, Robinson lunged at his assailant. A fourth shot whistled past him, but the police officer held on, striking Peace in the face.

Shouting, 'You b___, I will settle you this time,' Peace fired again and PC Robinson received a bullet to his right arm, just above the elbow. A scuffle ensued and Robinson managed to strike Peace on the head with his own firearm, which was strapped to the thief's wrist, rendering him unconscious. When Peace arrived at Greenwich police station, he gave his name as 'John Ward'.

Whilst in Newgate Prison awaiting the hearing, Peace received a visitor, Henry Fersey Brion, an inventor and friend with whom Peace had been collaborating on the development of some new patents for a number of inventions such as a helmet for firefighters, an extendable brush for washing railway carriages and a gas-filled contraption for raising sunken ships. Brion identified the prisoner as 'John Thompson', as that was the name under which he had known him. The police soon connected Peace to 'Mrs Thompson', but by then Susan had returned to Nottingham, where she changed her name back to 'Bailey'. Charlie's wife and family had also fled back to Sheffield, and when the police questioned Hannah Peace and her daughter they found stolen goods at their home. They finally identified the prisoner as Charlie Peace, who was still wanted for Arthur Dyson's murder, two years earlier.

On 18 November 1878, Charlie Peace was tried at the Old Bailey, under the name of John Ward, for burglary and the attempted murder of PC Robinson. He was found guilty and sentenced to life imprisonment. He was then transferred to Pentonville Prison, while the police built the case against him for Dyson's murder. On 16 January 1879, Peace was ordered to be removed to Sheffield to attend the preliminary hearing for the murder charge. Under heavy prison guard, he was returned to London that evening and then made the same journey by train to Sheffield the following day. This time, he managed to escape through the train window after asking to relieve himself. He fell onto the tracks and, before he could get away, the warders stopped the train and captured him. The proceedings were postponed.

A week later, Peace was transferred again to his home city, accompanied by even more guards. He was remanded to appear at the Leeds Assizes at the beginning of February, where he stood trial for murder before Mr Justice Lopes – a judge who had supported the campaign to spare William Habron in 1876. After just ten minutes' deliberation, the jury returned a guilty verdict and Charlie Peace was sentenced to death.

His execution was set for 25 February at Armley Gaol, but first he decided to make his final confession.

On 17 February 1879, Peace wrote a statement confessing to the murder of PC Nicholas Cock. He opened with the revelation that on 27 and 28 November 1876, he had been present at the Habron brothers' trial at the Manchester Assizes, after having read about their arrest in the newspapers. Peace then described how between seven and ten witnesses had testified against the defendants, all of whom he knew had perjured themselves, with the exception of one. He did not state who the only witness to speak the truth was, except that it was a civilian, rather than the police and it was not law student John Massey Simpson. He went on to describe what had really happened on the night of 1 August.

Charlie Peace was walking down Upper Chorlton Road towards Seymour Grove, with the intention of committing a burglary in the wealthy houses of the area, and as he turned the corner, he saw the police officers talking to two civilians, at the 'Ducking Stone [*sic*]', which marked the end of PC Cock's beat. Peace crossed the road and went into the grounds of a house. One of the police officers followed him and stood on the steps of the house with his bulls eye lantern switched on. Peace fled and, as he jumped over the wall, he saw the other police officer coming towards him. Fearing capture, he fired one chamber of his revolver 'to frighten him' but PC Cock continued to rush at him. He discharged another chamber and the bullet struck the officer in the chest. As he was shot, PC Cock 'threw up his walking stick saying "Ah! You b____r"' and fell to the ground.

Peace fled the scene by scaling a wall at the back of another house along the road. He ran across the field to Old Trafford railway station, where he entered the railway tunnel and walked on the track for about two miles, before reaching a road. As he made his escape, he saw only one person, who was working by a fire, but the man did not see him. He also heard a dog barking, as mentioned by those living near West Point.

In the final paragraph, Peace offered proof to support his confession: 'you will find that the ball was taken out of coxs brest is one of Haleys no 9 tinfire cartridge and was fired out of my revolver [*sic*].' His firearm was then being held at Leeds Town Hall and he suggested comparing the bullet in that gun with the one retrieved from PC Cock, to check if they weighed the same and both fit into the cartridge case. He ended his statement by saying, 'this man is inosent. I have don my duty and leve the rest to you [*sic*].' Peace had also drawn a map to illustrate the incident, on which he marked the spot where he encountered PC Cock, and his escape route.

Two days later, Peace asked with an interview with the prison governor, in the presence of Rev J.H. Littlewood, his former prison chaplain and later his vicar in Darnall as, according to the *Sheffield Daily Telegraph*, 'the convict had always had great confidence in him.' Peace made his final confession before the governor, Rev Littlewood, two prison warders and two other prison officials. The interview was reported in full in the local newspaper.

When Rev Littlewood arrived at the prison, Peace said that he was 'greatly gratified' to see him, as he wanted to unburden his mind, in the imminence of his death: 'I want to take from my conscience some things which weigh heavily upon it.' After pleading for reassurance that the clergyman would believe him, Peace began by stating that, as he had 'nothing to gain and nothing to lose', he wished to repent for his past life: 'if I could only undo what I have done, or make amends for it in any way I would suffer my body as I now stand to be cut in pieces inch by inch.' After clearing himself of a burglary that was committed at the home of the very vicar who was hearing his confession, and making a brief reference to the murder of Arthur Dyson, he described the night he killed PC Cock. This time, he embellished the account with more convincing detail.

Charlie Peace stated that he had come to Manchester in the summer of 1876, to 'work' some houses. He explained that he 'made a point of dressing respectably, as the police never think of suspecting anyone who appears in good clothes. In this way I have thrown the police off their guard many a time.'

He recounted how he had met the police officers on 1 August, while on his way to a target in Seymour Grove. Claiming that he still did not know the name of the murdered police officer, he described how he all but fell into his arms as he jumped off the wall. The officer made a grab for him: 'My blood was up, being nettled that I had been disturbed, so I said to him; "You stand back, or I'll shoot you."' Peace then paused in his account to reiterate that he had never intended to kill the officer: 'I always made it a rule that during the whole of my career never to take life if I could avoid it.' He never wanted to murder anyone, it was simply in order to get away: 'it does seem odd, after all, that in the end I should have to be hanged for having taken life – the very thing I was always so anxious to avoid.'

Peace fired wide but this did not discourage PC Cock: 'the policeman was as determined a man as myself.' This time, he disclosed that Cock had been about to strike him with his staff and that he had no time to lose if he wanted to escape. There was a scuffle and he fired a second time but was not able to take careful aim, and so shot Cock in the chest rather than the arm: 'I got away, which was all I wanted.' Soon after, Peace read about the Habron brothers' arrest in the press and decided to attend the assizes, fully aware that he was the real perpetrator: 'That interested me; I like to attend trials.' He watched as William was sentenced to death for his own crime, justifying his silence by saying that anyone in his position would have done the same: 'Some people will say that I was a hardened wretch for allowing an innocent man to suffer for my crime... Could I have done otherwise, knowing as I did that I should certainly be hanged for the crime?' The very next day he killed Arthur Dyson back in Sheffield.

In the interview Peace reiterated many times that he had not intended to murder either of the men. The real cause of their deaths, he claimed, was his missing his aim in the struggle to escape and 'accidentally committing murder'. He ended the interview by asking Rev Littlewood to hear his prayers and for 20 minutes he 'poured out fervent petitions for mercy', praying for Arthur Dyson and PC Cock, 'whose souls he launched into eternity without a moment's warning.'

Chapter 10

THE LAW'S DELAY

'If the publicity given to the infamous career of
Charles Peace can do no other good, it must serve
to fix public attention on the defects of the English
police, both as a protective and a detective force.'

(Lloyd's Weekly Newspaper, 9 February 1879)

According to the *Lloyd's Weekly Newspaper*, Charlie Peace
once encountered executioner William Marwood and, 'with
the grim humour of the hardened ruffian', asked him to grease
the rope 'should he ever fall into his professional hands'. The
next time they met, William Marwood was about to perform
his professional duty for the convicted murderer's execution,
at Armley Gaol on Tuesday 25 February 1879.

As executions had been held in private for just over a decade,
the only witnesses to Charlie Peace's hanging were the prison
officials, the under-sheriff and four invited representatives of
the press. The journalists then telegraphed the details of their
first-hand accounts to their colleagues and, the following day,
reports were published in national and regional newspapers,
such as the *London Evening Standard*, which described the
event in full.

The night before the execution, the prison chaplain visited
Peace in the condemned cell, at about 10.45 pm. After a short

time spent in prayer, he left the prisoner to rest. Not surprisingly, Charlie had difficulty sleeping and so the prison governor joined him and 'chatted very cheerfully' for 20 minutes, until 1 am. The chaplain then came for another hour, reporting that Peace 'was in a repentant frame of mind, and looked forward to his death with no great uneasiness or alarm'. He slept 'soundly and calmly' from the early hours of the morning until 5.45 am, when 'he appeared much refreshed by his few hours of undisturbed repose'. Peace had a hearty breakfast of toast, bacon, eggs and tea, after which the chaplain returned to stay with him until the hour of his execution. The prisoner 'exhibited much religious fervour and penitence.'

The gallows had been erected on the west side of the prison, near to the hospital wing, where the view was obscured by a high wall. The crowds had already gathered outside and, according to the *London Evening Standard*, all that could be heard was 'the hum of voices and the occasional laughter which the morning air wafted across the prison yard.' The scaffold was draped in black, with the earth excavated beneath it to a depth of three or four feet to accommodate the drop.

At 8 am, the solemn procession made its way to the place of execution, across the prison yard. Peace was wearing his convict dress and his arms had already been pinioned by Marwood in his cell. He refused help from the warders and walked unaided: 'The way in which he walked surprised everyone. His tread was firm and bold, and though he bowed his head, he had no apparent fear or nervousness, walking straight on.' As he approached, Peace could not see the gallows but as he turned sharply to the left, it came into view. He raised his face, which was wan and haggard, and his countenance became even paler: 'there was a startled look in his eyes, and his tread became less buoyant and firm, but the sensation of fear passed away almost as quickly as it came.' Reaching the foot of the scaffold he mounted the steps and stood beneath the beam, from which the noose was already hanging.

Marwood strapped his legs together and fastened the noose around his neck. He was about to place the cap over his head when Peace called out: 'Don't; I want to look.' After crying out to God for mercy, he asked if he could address the reporters:

'You know that my life has been base and bad. I wish you to show the world after you have seen my death, what man could die, as I am about to die, if he did not die in the fear of the Lord.' He went on to say how he felt that God had forgiven him, and that he wished his enemies well. Peace expressed his concern for his wife and children, that 'none will disgrace them by taunting or jeering them upon my account, but will have mercy on them.' After his final goodbyes, Marwood went to place the cap over his head again, and Peace interrupted, asking for a drink. His request was ignored and the ceremony continued. The chaplain said, 'Lord Jesus, receive his spirit,' and Marwood pulled the bolt. Charlie Peace fell through the trapdoor and disappeared from view.

Peace's body was left to hang on the gallows for about an hour, before Marwood cut it down, ready for the inquest, which confirmed that his death had been instantaneous – Marwood had done as Peace had asked and granted him a quick death. By this time, several hundred people were gathered outside the prison walls, despite the bitter cold. When the black flag was raised, 'a kind of shudder was observable amongst the people as the flag ascended, but the feeling soon passed away, and from a large number of the assembled crowd rose an inhuman shout.' However, Charlie Peace had the final word: he had designed his own funeral card, on which he had had printed, 'In memory of Charles Peace, who was executed in Armley Prison, Tuesday, Feb. 25, 1879, aged 47. For that I done, but never intended.'

After Peace's execution, the newspapers renewed their examination of his last-minute confession. Some suggested that he had revealed his crime due to a 'thirst for notoriety'. Others thought that it was an attempt to avenge himself on the police or that he had hoped for a respite whilst his claim was investigated. The fact that he had made his revelations in the presence of a priest suggested that it might have been a genuine act of penitence. Whatever Peace's motivation, attention soon returned to the Habron trial, the verdict of which still 'excited very general and serious misgivings'. With PC Cock's alleged killer now dead, William Habron's innocence still had to be proved, before he could be released.

Many people agreed that the original evidence had been entirely circumstantial and conflicting, and that the brothers had been arrested due to the previous charges of drunkenness, as well as the threats they had made against Constable Cock. It was acknowledged that the police had only started gathering the evidence after the arrest. Furthermore, the jury members had based their decision on Superintendent Bent's verbal description of the matching footprints, without having seen the marks for themselves. There was never any evidence that William Habron had carried a firearm, and the murder weapon had never been found, despite the police's indefatigable efforts. One source also observed that if the 'mystery man' seen under the gaslight that night by the two police officers, had been William Habron, then they should have recognised him instantly.

The general feeling was that the evidence in this case was cumulative, inferring rather than proving Habron's guilt. The judge had encouraged the jury to act in the interest of the general public, to assuage their fears of violence, and that the recommendation to mercy was an indication of their misgivings about the verdict. Furthermore, the Habron trial was a serious indictment of the British police force, which had already been undermined by Charlie Peace's crimes: 'The career of Charles Peace casts also a severe reflection on the English police. That it had been possible in spite of all our preventive and detective machinery is a fact which has not only affrighted society, but has more than justified the fright, by giving a direct and immediate stimulus to the burglar's trade,' the *Lloyd's Weekly Newspaper* fulminated. With little confidence now in the authorities' ability to serve justice for William Habron, his supporters clamoured for his pardon.

Following Peace's confession, Joseph Lomas, one of the campaign's leaders, wrote to the home secretary, enclosing letters from John Habron pleading for his brother's freedom. Lomas suggested that Peace's execution be postponed for William Habron's sake: 'Many people in this quarter think that you will not let Peace die until you are thoroughly satisfied as to his statement in connection with the Whalley Range murder' (as the case was referred to locally). He ended his letter with: I know that you will use your superior endeavour to sift out the truth.' However, Peace was now dead, and there had been no mention of a release for Habron.

Prior to the Habron case there had been a number of prosecutions involving clear misgivings over a guilty verdict, but there had been no official pardons for those convicted. There was no real incentive for the authorities to investigate the truth of a closed case, especially if the alleged offender had already been hanged. In 1815 Eliza Fenning had been executed for attempting to murder the family for whom she worked as a cook, by serving them arsenic-laced dumplings. After her death, speculation arose that the real killer was a member of the family and even Charles Dickens believed that her conviction had been a miscarriage of justice, but no action was taken and, after all, she was already dead.

Another sensational case in 1850 attracted attention. Nineteen-year-old William Ross was executed in York for the murder of his wife, having allegedly poisoned her with arsenic to claim the burial club money, a type of insurance commonly paid into by working class people against funeral costs. After his death, rumours circulated that his sister-in-law had been the true perpetrator but, once again, the case was never re-opened. Later in the century, after the Habron case, public opinion increasingly affected the outcome of high-profile cases. In 1899, Florence Maybrick was convicted of poisoning her husband, despite the circumstantial nature of the evidence against her. Like William Habron, her death sentence was commuted to life imprisonment, and she was eventually released 14 years later.

These cases fuelled the campaign for the abolition of capital punishment especially as, without modern forensic tools, it was difficult to prove guilt conclusively. As the century wore on, fewer criminals were executed and the ultimate sanction was more often replaced by transportation and later, life imprisonment. Had it not been for William Habron's ardent supporters like Joseph Lomas, it is uncertain whether the home secretary would have re-examined his case, even in the light of Charlie Peace's confession.

At the beginning of March, the Home Office began to

collect evidence, comprising the original trial documents, maps and sketches of the murder scene, and the details of Peace's confession. Marked 'pressing', the lengthy and detailed document was passed to the Law Office, in preparation for a conference on the matter. The presiding judge in the Habron trial, Mr Justice Lindley, proposed a further examination of the two bullets, the one removed from PC Cock's body and the one in Peace's firearm, which was immediately set in motion. Although the final report acknowledged that there had been some doubt in the verdict, Mr Justice Lindley was not prepared to admit that the jury's decision had been wrong or unsatisfactory, even though new evidence had now come to light. It was also noted that Habron's parents' petition had never questioned his guilt, but sought to commute his death sentence. The report concluded that the commutation of Habron's conviction was only possible if it was agreed that he was 'fully innocent' after a full review of the evidence.

On 13 March, Joseph Lomas wrote to the home secretary once again, stating that the brothers' long employment by Francis Deakin proved that they 'must have borne good or at least fair character'. He repeated the events of the day of the murder, with John's appearance in court, alleging that John had been 'thoroughly sober'. Lomas claimed that the police were 'acting in a strange manner throughout towards the Habrons', perhaps due to their anti-Irish prejudice, which had led to their frequent arrests. Lomas conceded that the footprints had belonged to William, and that they were probably made on his way home that night. He included a newspaper cutting with a statement made by one of the expert witnesses from the trial to support his claims. Boot warehouseman James Sturgess, had examined William's boots and found them to be 'ordinary, rough, country-made boots'. He had taken the boots back to West Point to compare them with the prints, but had found it 'totally impossible to get a perfect print' due to the path being composed of gravel and cinders. In his opinion, Superintendent Bent's footprint evidence was not admissible.

Lomas also reminded the home secretary that the bullet found in Cock's body and the one in Peace's rifle were 'of the same kind', which he had learnt from the expert gunsmith consulted by the court. He ended his letter by stating Habron's innocence: 'looking at the surroundings of this truly lamentable affair I can come to no other conclusion than that Habron is innocent of the crime for which he has been tried and convicted and who had a very narrow chance of being launched into eternity.' He implored the home secretary to advise Her Majesty 'to set the young man at liberty'.

The home secretary replied by return of post: 'We have come to the conclusion that there are strong grounds for believing that William Habron is innocent of the crime of which he was convicted.'

On 18 March, Prisoner C 1547 was moved from Portland Prison, where he had been working in the stone quarries for almost two years, back to Millbank. Handcuffed for most of the train journey from Weymouth railway station to London, he was not told the reason for his transfer, to prevent 'any outbreak of uproarious joy'. There was some confusion on his arrival at Millbank, and William was almost put to work picking oakum until the chief warder intervened. William was led to a waiting room, where he met Francis Deakin, who broke the news of his freedom. The *Illustrated Police News* recounted that, on receiving the information, Habron was, 'singularly free from Celtic excitability'. The newspaper also described his appearance when he was finally released from prison: 'William Habron is by no means an ill-looking young Irishman, fresh-coloured and grey eyed.' He was wearing a dark suit, with his closely-cropped hair concealed beneath a billycock hat. Below average height, but well-built, 'he speaks with an Irish accent by no means strongly marked' and was considered to be 'respectful and singularly undemonstrative in his manner'.

On his release, William made a statement asserting his innocence and his confidence that 'an innocent man will never be allowed to suffer for the guilty.' However, he felt some resentment that he had not had the opportunity to improve himself whilst in prison: 'Nothing makes me so sorry as my lost time. Here I come out of prison as ignorant and helpless as I went in.' Since the 1865 Prison Act, instruction in the basic skills of reading, writing and arithmetic was provided in prisons. Inmates were assessed on entry against the standards set for primary school pupils and those deemed as having unsatisfactory levels of literacy and numeracy received two half-an hour lessons a week. Even though, on the calendar of prisoners, William's education was marked as 'imperfect', it is unclear why he did not receive any instruction in prison.

The following day, William travelled with his former employer back to Manchester, where he enjoyed a 'very affecting' reunion with his brothers, John and Frank. They gave him the tragic news that their father had died six months earlier of a 'broken heart', as was reported in the newspapers. The next day, all three brothers left for Ireland, crossing from Holyhead to Dublin and then travelling onto their home village of Cloonfad in County Roscommon, where they were met by the local brass band. That night the villagers lit bonfires in their honour.

After William Habron had been officially pardoned, the home secretary arranged for him to receive £1,000 in compensation (worth over £90,000 today), which was to be placed in the hands of two trustees, the Bishop of Salford and Francis Deakin. When William returned to Ireland, they paid him £200, with which he bought a farm near his mother. The trustees then invested the remaining £800 in the Salford Corporation. William remained in Ireland for the rest of the year, returning to the mainland in 1880, a trip which caused Francis Deakin some concern.

On 26 February, Francis Deakin wrote once more to the home secretary, informing him that William had been engaged by a theatrical agent in Bradford, to undertake a tour 'for public exhibition'. Disapproving strongly of this venture, Francis had advised William to 'remain quiet', but 'at last he has become disobedient'. He did not seek the home secretary's advice on the matter, but ended by reassuring him that most of the money paid in compensation was still safely invested. Deakin enclosed a newspaper cutting from the *Sheffield Daily Telegraph* about William's appearances in the city.

William Habron of 'Whalley Range murder notoriety' appeared for six nights at the Royal Pavilion Music Hall in Sheffield, in aid of 'the distressed in Ireland'. Food shortages were still causing poverty and hardship there at the end of the 1870s, particularly in the west of the country, where William's family lived. The auditorium was packed out, with many of those present 'not usually seen at this place of resort'. His jacket adorned with three medals with green ribbons, a symbol of Irish nationalism, Habron was led onto the stage by 'a countryman of his'. He smiled at the crowd, who greeted him with loud cheering. Both men bowed and William sat down on a chair, whilst his companion spoke on his behalf. 'With considerable fluency and at some length', the agent explained how Habron had forfeited his life for 'doing what he never did'. He described how Charlie Peace had confessed to the shooting of Constable Cock, which had led to Habron's release. The speaker explained that William had left his homeland again 'to help his suffering people'. He then took the silent Habron by the hand, they bowed and left the stage.

The review in the *Sheffield Daily Telegraph* concluded that the performance would have been more effective had William Habron spoken some words, or even read out a statement. Sitting on his chair, where he occasionally smiled or nodded his head, he was completely overshadowed by his agent, who was 'a gentleman of somewhat commanding presence', with 'a fluent style of oratory'. William's theatrical career was short-lived and, although he retained his farm in Ireland, he settled later in Ancoats, Manchester where he ran a beerhouse. In 1884, he appeared in Manchester Police Court again, and was convicted of a brutal assault, for which he was fined £25 and costs.

Since William Habron's conviction for PC Cock's murder, Superintendent James Bent had continued leading the Manchester Division of the Lancashire Constabulary. In 1879, another of his officers was injured, this time whilst on duty in Moss Side. Following reports of robberies, Bent had placed a number of officers in plain clothes in the area. In the early hours of one morning, Constable Leesdale followed a suspicious-looking man, 'wearing goloshes [*sic*]'. When the police officer tried to grab him, the man pulled a knife and stabbed PC Leesdale in the hand. Another officer came to his assistance and struck the assailant on the head. After the police discovered a number of burglars' tools in the prisoner's house, he was convicted and received ten years' penal servitude. This time the police officer survived the attack.

The following year, however, Superintendent Bent investigated another ambiguous murder, for which he once again used a very controversial method of identifying the killer. At 9 pm on 7 January 1880, Sergeant Lever rushed into Old Trafford Police Station to report a 'dreadful murder', which had taken place in Harpurhey, an industrial suburb in north-east Manchester. Superintendent Bent went straight to the house, where he found 19-year-old maid Sarah Jane Roberts lying dead in a pool of blood, with several 'fearful' wounds to the head. There were no signs of a struggle but her right forearm bore a mark, presumably from being raised in self-defence. The householder, Mr Greenwood, had been absent from the house, when the crime was committed, but his bed-ridden wife had been upstairs. She had heard a knock at the door, followed soon after by a terrible scream.

Originally from Oswestry, Sarah Jane Roberts had been working for the Greenwoods for about a year. There was no obvious motive for her brutal murder. Pressure mounted to find her killer and Superintendent Bent resorted to having the victim's eyes photographed, in case the attacker's face was imprinted on them. The day before Sarah Jane's funeral the police lifted the coffin lid and took images of the corpse, in the hope that the figure of the murderer would appear under the examination of a powerful microscope. Despite the image being magnified to the size of half a sheet of ordinary notepaper: 'there was nothing visible which would furnish the slightest evidence as to the features of the murderer' (*Manchester Courier*, 16 January 1880). Sarah Jane's killer was never caught.

In 1891, while serving on the force, Superintendent Bent published his memoirs. In a chapter devoted to PC Cock's murder, he described the case from his perspective, giving a first-hand account of the events leading up to the shooting, the investigation and trial. He blamed William Habron's conviction on the contradictory statements made by the witnesses for the defence, rather than 'any evidence given by the police'.

However, Bent claimed he was satisfied with Habron's release: 'he had not a friend in the world more pleased to hear of his release than I was' and he reported that William had visited him at home several times since. James Bent continued to work as a police officer until his death on 8 July 1901, at the age of 73.

Often perceived as a harsh and uncompromising police officer whilst he was alive, James Bent is now remembered for his compassion for Manchester's poverty-stricken children. Touched by the plight of the many starving individuals he encountered, especially young people living in the most miserable of conditions, he opened a soup kitchen in the drill hall of Old Trafford police station in 1878. At its height, the kitchen served 150,000 meals a year to the poorest children in Manchester and Salford. Bent and his staff also provided the children with clothes and clogs, taking them on boat trips and picnics. Superintendent Bent's charitable work is commemorated with a blue plaque near to the former site of the soup kitchen in Old Trafford.

Almost 140 years since his death, notorious burglar and murderer Charlie Peace is well-recorded in the annals of crime history. Shortly after his execution, the *Illustrated Police News* published a photograph of the tools he used to carry out his crimes, including a pole with a hook for climbing walls and the toothbrushes with which he dyed his hair. One of his violins – allegedly Peace had many – was sold at auction and, in 1965, it was offered to the Metropolitan Police Crime Museum for preservation. This particular violin was made in about 1820, and is of French origin, with a German bow. Its previous owner, a Mrs E. Trueman from Newbury, sold the violin in 1957. She also owned the green baize bag in which, according to her, Peace carried the instrument when travelling by train, and in which her mother kept clothes pegs. Mrs Trueman had inherited the violin from her great-grandfather, a Yorkshire shoemaker. Together with his folding ladder, Charlie Peace's violin is now held at the Crime Museum at New Scotland Yard.

PC Nicholas Cock is also still remembered. In 1956, his headstone was removed from the churchyard on Chorlton Green and placed at the headquarters of the Lancashire

Constabulary near Preston, for safekeeping. All that remains in the churchyard now is a simple plaque on the ground, bearing his name, age (which is incorrect) and the date he was killed. To this day, Greater Manchester Police officers stop by his stone to pay their respects whilst on their beat in Chorlton-cum-Hardy.

Further Reading

BOOKS:

Bent, James, *Criminal Life: Reminiscences of Forty-Two Years as a Police Officer* (John Hayward, 1891)

Hayes, Cliff, *Manchester Photographic Memories* (2000, The Francis Frith Collection)

Cooper, Glynis, *The Illustrated History of Manchester's Suburbs* (2002, Breedon Books)

Hayhurst, Alan, *Greater Manchester Murders* (The History Press, 2009)

Johnson, Ben, *Charlie Peace: Murder, Mayhem and the Master of Disguise* (Pen and Sword Books, 2016)

Kidd, Alan, *Manchester: A History* (Carnegie Publishing, 1993)

O'Neill Joseph, *Crime City: Manchester's Victorian Underworld* (2008, Milo Books)

O'Neill, Joseph, *The Manchester Martyrs* (The Mercier Press Ltd, 2013)

Simpson, Andrew, *The Story of Chorlton-cum-Hardy* (The History Press, 2012)

NEWSPAPERS:

Illustrated Police News, 1879
Lloyd's Weekly Newspaper, 1876, 1879, 1898
London Daily News, 1876
London Evening Standard, 1879
Manchester Courier, 1876
Manchester Guardian, 1876
Manchester Times, 1876
Pall Mall Gazette, 1876
Police Gazette, 1876
Sheffield Daily Telegraph, 1879, 1880

ARCHIVES:

The National Archives, Kew – HO 144/23/60198; TS 18/2;
MEPO 2/10501

Acknowledgements

I am very fortunate to have the support of such a wonderful publishing team and I would like to thank my editor Jen Boyle, my cover designer Jessica Bell, and my formatter, Linda White. I would also like to thank my loyal writing partner and friend, Rachael Hale, who is always my first reader and has a very perceptive red pen. I would like to thank friends Lindsay Siviter and Linda Stratmann for their fantastic support, and for sharing information and images about the case.

Many thanks also to the staff at the National Archives at Kew – I am always impressed by the excellent service there, as well as the treasure trove of unique documents. Although much research is now undertaken online, there is nothing more exciting and special than holding a document such as the crumbling confession written by Charlie Peace in your hand.

I love my work as a 21st century 'detective' investigating Victorian crime, and I am extremely grateful to my faithful readers – I couldn't do this work without you. Huge thanks to all those who read my cases, attend my talks and chat about crime with me via social media. Thank you for buying my latest true crime case and if you would like to support me further, please leave a short review on Amazon, Goodreads, or wherever you can – thank you! If you would like to find out more about my sleuthing work, you can join my Crime Club for free. You will receive regular updates through my newsletter, as well as free giveaways and samples. You can sign up on my website:

www.angelabuckleywriter.com

Finally, I would like to thank my parents for providing me with a happy childhood home, near a historic crime scene!

About the Author

Angela's life of crime began with her own shady ancestors who struggled to survive in the dangerous slums of Victorian Manchester. Her first book was *The Real Sherlock Holmes: The Hidden Story of Jerome Caminada* (Pen and Sword, 2014). *Amelia Dyer and the Baby Farm Murders*, was the first in her new historical true crime series, Victorian Supersleuth Investigates. *Who Killed Constable Cock?* is the second.

Angela has shared stories of Victorian crime in national magazines and newspapers, at literary festivals and events, and on BBC radio and television. She has appeared on The One Show, Mysteries at the Museum and BBC One South Today. Angela's work has featured in *The Times*, *The Telegraph*, the *Sunday Express, All About History, Who Do You Think You Are? Magazine* and *Your Family History*. She is a member of the Crime Writers' Association.

Originally from Manchester, Angela's childhood home was close to the spot where PC Nicholas Cock was killed in 1876.

You can find out more about Angela's work at www. angelabuckleywriter.com and follow her on Twitter @ amebuckley, on Facebook on her Victorian Supersleuth page and on Instagram as victoriansupersleuth

Amelia Dyer and the Baby Farm Murders

As featured in the Reading Year of Culture and on BBC One South Today

On 30 March 1896, a bargeman hooked a parcel from the river Thames at Caversham. Inside the brown paper package was the body of a baby girl – she had been strangled with tape. When two more tiny bodies were found in a carpet bag, the police launched a nationwide hunt for a serial killer.

A faint name and address on the sodden wrapping provided Reading police with their first clue. Can Chief Constable George Tewsley and his colleagues catch this heartless baby farmer before more infants meet a similar fate?

'A gripping tale of Victorian detective work' – *Your Family History* magazine

'The spine-chilling tale of how Reading became home to one of the 19th century's most notorious criminals' – *Reading Chronicle*

The Real Sherlock Holmes

The Hidden Story of Jerome Caminada

As seen in The Telegraph, The Times and on The One Show

A master of disguise with a keen eye for detail and ingenious methods of deduction, Detective Caminada pursued notorious criminals through the seedy streets of Victorian Manchester's underworld. Known as a 'terror to evil-doers', he stalked pickpockets and thieves, ruthless con artists and cold-blooded killers.

Bearing all the hallmarks of Sir Arthur Conan Doyle, this compelling story establishes Detective Caminada as a true Victorian super-sleuth and a real-life Sherlock Holmes.

'A gripping new book' – Manchester Evening News

'A treat for inquisitive readers' – The Crime Readers' Association

'A highly enjoyable book' – The Whitechapel Society

Printed in Poland
by Amazon Fulfillment
Poland Sp. z o.o., Wrocław